Chocolate

Chocolate

cakes, cookies, candies and more

A Fireside Book
Published by Simon & Schuster
New York   London   Toronto   Sidney

Summary

A Sweet Vice

A true icon of pleasure for any sweet-toothed hedonist, chocolate has long been a favorite with the world's top pastry chefs because of its great adaptability. One of the few luxuries in life that is accessible to all, the ultimate guiltless pleasure – if consumed in small doses it is even said to be healthy! Chocolate is a nutritious food, rich in beneficial properties and offering a wealth of sensual pleasures.

Tropical Origins

Initially, chocolate was known as a rather bitter drink, chocolátl, enjoyed by pre-Colombian civilizations. The drink was made from the beans of the cacao plant and various spices such as chile pepper. Some archeological finds lead us to believe that the cacao plant and beverage were well known and widely consumed as early as 600 AD.

One anecdote recounts that the Aztec emperor Montezuma drank up to 40 cups of chocolátl every day in order to benefit from the already recognized properties of the cacao beans. In fact, chocolátl was held to have reinvigorating qualities, due to the high level of theobromine in the beans. Due to its mystic and religious significance, the beverage was consumed by pre-Colombian priests during important ceremonies and offered to the gods. Not by chance, the cacao plant was later classified by the naturalist Linnaeus as Theobroma cacao, from the Greek word for "food of the gods." The importance of cacao was so great that its beans were used as a monetary unit and measurement in pre-Colombian civilizations.

The first Conquistadors immediately realized the significance of cacao to these societies. They were also taken with the plant's spectacular beauty: a lush tree with brightly colored pods covering entire tracts of the tropical forests, an impressive sight to the European explorers.

a little history

It is estimated that the production of cocoa today has grown a thousand fold since the 1800s. In just two centuries, cocoa production has changed considerably. The major cocoa-producing countries at the beginning of the 19th century were Venezuela and Ecuador. With new distribution systems the largest cocoa producers are now the Ivory Coast, Ghana and Indonesia, providing about 75% of the world's cocoa.

The Origins of Modern Chocolate

When chocolate first arrived in Europe in the 16th century, it was considered just one of the many novel products imported from the New World. The recipe for the mysterious chocolate drink consumed by pre-Colombian civilizations was kept secret in the kitchens of the Spanish royal court. Like all novelties, it took time and modification for chocolate to be widely appreciated and grow into the rich legend that it is today. Spanish monks were the first to experiment with chocolate, mixing it with other herbs in infused drinks. They adapted the original recipes, making the Mayan chocolate drink more palatable to European tastes. Cocoa butter, vanilla and sugar were added to soften the excessive bitter flavors, and pepper and chile were removed completely.

The major change to chocolate production and distribution came in 1828 when Conrad J. Van Houten, a Dutch chemist, invented a process that pulverized the cacao beans into something similar to modern cocoa powder. Before Van Houten's invention, cacao beans were still ground and processed using a technique very similar to the one used by the pre-Colombian civilizations. Spices, sugar and cocoa butter were then added to the semi-liquid paste obtained. Occasionally flour was added to the mixture to thicken and homogenize the drink's consistency.

From Cacao to Chocolate

Criollo, Forastero and Trinitario are the three main categorizations into which cacao varieties are divided. Trinitario is a hybrid obtained from the Criollo and Forastero varieties. There are two other outstanding classifications, Porcelana and Chuao, which are very rare but have an exceptional flavor. The essential differences between the various cacao varieties are in the seed shape and the aroma of the cocoa, which takes on different flavors depending on the soil and climate where the plant was grown.

suggestion

To fully appreciate the flavor of chocolate – dark, milk or flavored – we suggest pairing it with an excellent espresso coffee or coffee prepared in a moka pot. The coffee used should be aromatic, creamy and of course served very hot.

chocolate

7

Native to the tropical regions of Central and South America, today the cocoa plant is also grown in Africa, Indonesia and western India. Chocolate production begins on plantations in the wet and humid tropical forest areas. Cacao plants require a specific humid, rainy climate for ideal growth, with temperatures between 64° and 90°F (18° to 32°C).

Theobroma cacao plants normally grow in the shade of a taller tree, often called the "cocoa mother." The mother tree protects the cacao plant from the harsh tropical sun, especially in the early stages of growth. Fruit is harvested from the cacao trees twice a year, with the first harvest producing higher quality yields. When the fruit pod reaches maturity it is cut from the tree and chopped open with a machete, and the beans and pulp collected.

The seeds are then fermented at a temperature around 120°F (50°C) to remove the gelatinous white membrane that covers the beans.

Finally, the beans are sun-dried to protect against humidity mold. In particularly humid countries, the beans are dried on cedar boards in special hot-air cupboards.

After the drying process, the cacao beans are toasted in a process similar to coffee roasting. Toasting the beans facilitates the next stage in the process in which the shells are removed. The beans are then smashed into small granules. Finally, the granules are ground until they melt into a fluid mass (also called chocolate liquor). At this point, the cocoa may be processed in several ways depending on the final use.

■ **Types of Chocolate:** chocolate is generally classified by the percentage of cocoa it contains. Here is a brief summary of the most common types of chocolate.

■ **Couverture:** usually found in professional kitchens, this chocolate must be tempered before use. It is an excellent material for confectionery as it provides

a curiosity
Crus are the latest trend among chocolate connoisseurs. A chocolate cru comes from only from cacao plants grown in a single, specified geographic area.
Just like wines, some particularly fine chocolates can be labeled "Grand Cru" or "Vintage."

a smooth covering. Couverture may be made with dark, milk or white chocolate, and is often paired with other ingredients according to the pastry chef's tastes and imagination.

■ **Superior Grade Dark Chocolate:** also called extra-fine, it must have a cocoa content of at least 43%. Extra-dark chocolate must have at least 45% cocoa. Today dark chocolate is made in many varying strengths, from the most moderate with the minimum cocoa percentages to intermediate varieties (60-70% cocoa) to a few very strong types which reach up to 99% cocoa.

■ **Milk Chocolate:** a classic, the most popular of the chocolate types and a favorite with children. Usually milk or its derivatives, cream, butter and butyric acid, are added to the chocolate.
Milk chocolate contains at least 25% cocoa, 14% milk derivatives and 3.5% butyric acid. The sucrose content must be no higher than 55%.
Like dark chocolate, milk chocolate also comes in superior or extra-fine versions which contain more cocoa (at least 30%), 18% milk products and 4.5% butyric acid.
Superior quality milk chocolates are higher in fat but generally tastier than the regular kind.

■ **Giandula Chocolate:** a mix of chocolate (at least 32% cocoa) and ground hazelnuts, with variants using almonds or walnuts.

■ **White Chocolate:** containing sucrose (maximum 55%), cocoa butter (at least 20%) and milk or powdered milk derivatives (at least 14%), regulations prevent white chocolate from using color additives.
Although it is called "chocolate," it does not actually contain any chocolate liquor or cocoa solids.

did you know...
Cocoa powder comes from the processing of cocoa solids. Unsweetened cocoa powder can be either natural, which is more bitter, with a deep chocolate flavor, or Dutch-process, which has been treated with an alkali to remove the acids and has more delicate taste.

contents

Milk and White

dark chocolate cakes

chocolate

duchess cake

Ingredients for 6 servings

Cake:

1 cup plus 2 tbsps (9 oz or 250 g) butter

2 cups (9 oz or 250 g)
confectioners' sugar

1⅓ cups (9 oz or 250 g) hazelnuts,
toasted, peeled and finely chopped

2 cups (9 oz or 250 g) all-purpose flour

Sabayon:

8 egg yolks, **1** cup (7 oz or 200 g) sugar

2/3 cup (150 ml) dry Marsala wine

3 tbsps white wine

Chocolate cream:

5 egg yolks, zest from 1 organic lemon

2/3 cup (4½ oz or 130 g) sugar

1½cups (350 ml) milk

1/2 vanilla bean, halved lengthwise

9 oz (250 g) dark chocolate

4 tbsps (2 oz or 50 g) butter

Cream together the butter, confectioners' sugar and hazelnuts. Add the flour and mix to obtain a smooth dough. Refrigerate for 2-3 hours.
Preheat the oven to 400°F (200°C or Gas Mark 6). Roll out the dough and cut it into 3 rounds. Place the rounds on a buttered baking sheet and bake for 5 minutes. Make the sabayon: Whisk together all of the ingredients over a double boiler. Cook over medium heat, whisking constantly, until thick and smooth. Make the chocolate cream: Beat the egg yolks with the sugar. Bring the milk to a boil with the lemon zest and vanilla bean. Remove from heat, strain and whisk into the egg mixture. Return to the saucepan and cook over medium heat, stirring with a whisk, until thick. Remove from heat and cool completely. Melt the chocolate together with the butter and fold it into the cooled cream. Place 1 cake round on a serving plate. Spread it with a layer of chocolate cream, cover with another cake round and top with the sabayon. Add the remaining cake round and cover with the remaining chocolate cream. Decorate the cake, if desired, with confectioners' sugar and candied cherries.

Preparation time **30 minutes**
Cooking time **40 minutes**
Level **medium**

apricot and pine nut cake
with chocolate sauce

Ingredients for 6 servings
Cake:
2½ cups (11 oz or 310 g)
all-purpose flour
1 cup (250 ml) orange juice
1 cup plus 2 tbsps (9 oz or 250 g) butter
1¼ cups (250 g) sugar
3/4 cup (7 oz or 200 g) dried apricots,
chopped
3/4 cup (3½ oz or 100 g) pine nuts
grated zest and juice
of 2 organic oranges
3 eggs
1 tsp baking powder
Sauce:
3½ oz (100 g) dark chocolate
5 tbsps heavy cream

Preheat the oven to 325°F (170°C or Gas Mark 3).
Toast the pine nuts in the oven or in a non-stick frying pan for a few minutes. Let cool and coarsely chop.
Cream the softened butter with the sugar and orange zest. Sift in the flour and baking powder little by little, stirring constantly. Add the pine nuts, dried apricots and orange juice. Stir to combine, forming a smooth batter.
Pour the batter into a cake pan lined with parchment paper and bake for 1 hour 20 minutes.
Let cool for 15 minutes before unmolding the cake.
Melt the chocolate with the cream. Pour the hot chocolate sauce over slices of cake before serving.

To keep the apricots from sinking to the bottom of the cake while baking, coat them with a little flour before adding them to the batter.

Preparation time **30 minutes**
Cooking time **1 hour 25 minutes**
Level **easy**

chocoate pear tart

Ingredients for 4 servings
Crust:
1⅓ cups (6 oz or 165 g)
all-purpose flour
1/4 cup (1 oz or 30 g) ground almonds
2 tbsps (1 oz or 30 g) sugar
3-4 tbsps water, salt
9 tbsps (4½ oz or 125 g) butter
Filling:
4-5 ripe pears, **1** egg
1 cup (7 oz or 200 g) raw cane sugar
6 tbsps (3 oz or 90 g) butter
1/2 cup (1½ oz or 45 g) cocoa powder
1/3 cup (1½ oz or 45 g)
all-purpose flour
1 tsp vanilla extract
Decoration:
confectioners' sugar

The ground almonds may be substituted with 10 crumbled amaretto cookies and the zest of 1 orange.

Place the flour, sugar, ground almonds, water and salt in a large mixing bowl. Work in the butter with the fingertips until the mixture resembles a coarse meal. Continue to mix with a fork and then transfer the dough to a work surface and knead with the hands
Form the dough into a ball and cover with plastic wrap. Refrigerate for 30 minutes. Preheat the oven to 350°F (180°C or Gas Mark 4).
Roll out the dough into a thin sheet.
Line a round tart pan with the dough and refrigerate. Peel, quarter and core the pears. Remove the tart crust from the refrigerator and pierce it with a fork. Sprinkle with 2 tablespoons of sugar and top with the pears.
Bake for 15 minutes. Remove from the oven and let cool. Meanwhile, melt the butter with the cocoa powder in a saucepan. Stir until smooth. Beat the egg with the remaining sugar, add the butter mixture and sift in the flour. Add the vanilla and mix well. Pour the mixture over the pear tart and smooth with a spatula. Bake for another 15 minutes. Remove from the oven and cool completely. Sprinkle with confectioners' sugar and serve.

Preparation time **40 minutes**
Cooking time **30 minutes**
Level **medium**

bitter chocolate
and almond torte

Ingredients for 6 servings

Cake:

4 eggs, separated

1/2 cup (3 1/2 oz or 100 g) sugar

6½ tbsps all-purpose flour

1 tbsp cornstarch

3/4 cup (2½ oz or 75 g) unsweetened cocoa powder

1 tsp almond extract

1 tsp vanilla extract

salt

Decoration:

cocoa powder

Preheat the oven to 375°F (190°C or Gas Mark 5).
Beat the egg yolks and sugar in a mixing bowl and sift
in the flour, cornstarch and cocoa powder.
Mix well and add the almond extract and vanilla.
Beat the egg whites and a pinch of salt to stiff peaks.
Fold the egg whites into the cocoa and egg mixture.
Line a cake pan with parchment paper and pour
in the batter. Bake for 35 minutes. Remove from the oven
and let cool slightly. Invert the cake onto a serving dish
and sift cocoa powder over the cake. Serve warm.

Cakes

20

This cake may be served with a crème anglais or a little whipped cream if desired.

Preparation time **35 minutes**
Cooking time **35 minutes**
Level **easy**

flourless chili-chocolate torte

Ingredients for 6 servings

Cake:

10½ oz (300 g) dark chocolate, chopped

9 tbsps (4½ oz or 125 g) butter

6 eggs, separated

3/4 cup (5½ oz or 150 g) sugar

6 tbsps grappa

1/2 tsp ground chili pepper

Decoration:

unsweetened cocoa powder

Preheat the oven to 350°F (180°C or Gas Mark 4). Melt the chocolate and the butter over a double boiler. Beat the egg yolks with 1/2 cup (3½ oz or 100 g) of the sugar until thick and foamy. Whisk the melted chocolate into the egg mixture; add the grappa and chili pepper. Stir to combine.

Beat the egg whites with the remaining sugar to stiff peaks. Fold them into the chocolate mixture. Transfer the batter into a buttered, floured cake pan. Bake for 30 minutes, then lower the oven temperature to 225°F (110°C or Gas Mark 1/4) and bake for another 10 minutes. Remove from the oven, let cool for a few minutes and then unmold the cake. Let cool completely. Dust with cocoa powder before serving.

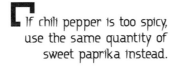

If chili pepper is too spicy, use the same quantity of sweet paprika instead.

Preparation time **20 minutes**
Cooking time **40 minutes**
Level **easy**

chocolate-hazelnut bundt cake

Ingredients for 8 servings

Cake:

4 eggs, separated

1/2 cup (3½ oz or 100 g) sugar

6½ oz (180 g) dark chocolate

3 tbsps (1½ oz or 50 g) butter

3/4 cup (1½ oz or 50 g) ground hazelnuts or hazelnut paste

3 tbsps all-purpose flour

3 tbsps cornstarch, salt

Decoration:

1/2 cup (120 ml) whipping cream

1/2 tbsp confectioners' sugar

5 mint leaves, raspberries (optional)

For the raspberry sauce: Puree 2½ cups 10½ oz or 300 g) of raspberries with 1 tablespoon of raw cane sugar and a few drops of lemon juice. Strain the mixture after pureeing to create a smooth, seedless sauce.

Preheat the oven to 350°F (180°C or Gas Mark 4). Beat the egg yolks with the sugar until foamy. Melt the chocolate and the butter over a double boiler or in the microwave. Stir the chocolate into the egg mixture. Add the hazelnuts and sift in the flour and cornstarch. Beat the egg whites and a pinch of salt to stiff peaks and fold them into the batter. Butter and flour a fluted Bundt pan and fill with the batter. Bake for 45 minutes. Let cool and invert onto a serving plate. Whip the cream. Decorate the cake with the whipped cream, confectioners' sugar, mint leaves and a puree of fresh raspberries if desired.

Preparation time **15 minutes**
Cooking time **45 minutes**
Level **easy**

dark chocolate bundt cake

Ingredients for 4 servings
Cake:

4 medium potatoes (1¾ lb or 800 g)

7 tbsps (3½ oz or 100 g) butter

1 cup plus 2 tbsps (8 oz or 225 g) sugar

1 tsp vanilla

1 cup (3½ oz or 100 g) ground almonds

grated zest of 1 orange

4 eggs, separated

4½ oz (125 g) dark chocolate

salt

Preheat the oven to 350°F (180°C or Gas Mark 4).
Boil the potatoes for 30 minutes.
Drain, peel and mash them with a ricer. Let cool.
Melt the butter and add it to the potatoes. Mix well.
Add the sugar, vanilla, ground almonds and grated orange zest. Mix well. Add the egg yolks. Shave the chocolate into the batter. Beat the egg whites with a pinch of salt to firm peaks. Fold the whites into the batter. Pour the mixture into a buttered Bundt pan. Place the pan in a baking dish and fill it half-full with hot water.
Bake for 45 minutes. Let the cake cool slightly and invert onto a serving dish.

When making desserts with beaten egg whites, make sure that the egg whites are beaten just before incorporating them into the batter so they do not lose their consistency.

Preparation time **20 minutes**
Cooking time **1 hour 20 minutes**
Level **easy**

flourless chocolate cake with rum jelly and eucalyptus foam

Ingredients for 6 servings

Flourless:

1 oz (25 g) dark chocolate (90% cocoa), chopped

7 tbsps (3½ oz or 100 g) butter

2 eggs, at room temperature

1/3 plus 1 tbsp (50 g) confectioners' sugar

1 tsp agar agar powder

1/2 cup (120 ml) aged rum

4 tbsps whipping cream

1 pinch ground eucalyptus leaves eucalyptus leaves (optional)

Agar agar powder is derived from a kind of red seaweed and is used as a thickening agent. It has a delicate flavor and is rich in minerals. It is often used to prepare gelatins and aspics as it does not affect the flavor of the ingredients.

Preheat the oven to 350°F (180°C or Gas Mark 4). Melt the chocolate in a double boiler or in the microwave. Cut the butter into small pieces and gradually stir it into the hot chocolate. Whisk in the eggs and the confectioners' sugar. Whisk until the mixture is smooth and shiny. Butter and flour a loaf pan and pour in the batter. Bake for 45 minutes. Meanwhile, dissolve the agar agar powder in a little rum and then add it to the remaining rum. Refrigerate until the jelly is set. Heat the half of the whipping cream with the crushed eucalyptus leaves then remove from the heat and let cool. Strain the infusion and add the remaining cream. Whisk until stiff, then refrigerate. Unmold the chocolate cake and slice it thickly. Chop the rum jelly into cubes. Serve the cake with the rum jelly and eucalyptus cream. If desired, decorate with eucalyptus leaves and serve with a tiny glass of rum.

Preparation time **20 minutes**
Cooking time **50 minutes**
Level **medium**

dome cake with chocolate glaze

Ingredients for 4 servings

Cake:

1⅓ cup (7 oz or 200 g) almonds

8 bitter almonds

3/4 cup (5½ oz or 150 g) finely ground semolina

grated zest of 1 organic lemon

6 eggs, separated

salt

1 cup (7 oz or 200 g) sugar

Glaze:

5½ oz (150 g) dark chocolate

2 tbsps (1 oz or 30 g) butter

Preheat the oven to 400°F (200°C or Gas Mark 6).
Soak all of the almonds in boiling water for 5 minutes.
Drain and dry in a clean kitchen towel. Rub the almonds
in the towel to remove the skins. Grind the almonds using
a mortar and pestle. Transfer to a mixing bowl and add
the semolina and lemon zest. Mix to combine.
Beat the egg whites and a pinch of salt to stiff peaks
and fold them into the almond mixture.
Add the egg yolks one at a time and then the sugar.
Mix carefully until the batter is smooth. Line a spherical or
bombe mold with aluminum foil and fill it with the batter.
Bake for 45 minutes. Remove from the oven and invert
the cake onto a piece of parchment paper.
Let sit for 24 hours.
Melt the chocolate and butter over a double boiler, mixing
well to combine. Spread the chocolate glaze over the base
of the cake. Let harden and then turn the cake over.
Pour the remaining glaze over the top of the cake.
Let harden before serving.

The semolina flour may be replaced
with the same quantity of finely
ground cornmeal, which will give the
cake a sweet fragrance.

Preparation time **40 minutes**
Cooking time **45 minutes**
Level **medium**

chocolate cake with pears

Ingredients for 6 servings

Cake:

3 pears

2 eggs, separated

1 egg yolk

1/2 cup plus 1 tbsp (110 g) sugar

9 oz (250 g) mascarpone

3/4 cup plus 1 tbsp (100 g) all-purpose flour

1/3 cup (1 oz or 35 g) cocoa powder

1/2 tsp baking powder

Decoration:

pear slices

Preheat the oven to 350°F (180°C or Gas Mark 4). Peel, core and dice the pears. Place in a bowl and set aside. Beat the egg yolks, whites and sugar with a whisk until foamy and bright yellow.
Add the mascarpone and mix well to obtain a smooth cream.Sift in the flour, cocoa powder and baking soda and stir to combine. Mix in the diced pears. Line a cake pan with parchment paper and pour in the batter.
Bake for 40 minutes. Invert the cake onto a serving plate. Serve the cake sliced, decorated with a few slices of pear.

Cakes

32

To keep the pears from turning brown, toss them with the juice of 1/2 lemon after dicing them. Alchermes or any other sweet liqueur may be used for the same purpose.

Preparation time **20 minutes**
Cooking time **40 minutes**
Level **easy**

glazed chocolate cake

Ingredients for 8 servings

Biscuit:

14 tbsps (7 oz or 200 g) butter, softened

1 cup (7 oz or 200 g) sugar

2 cups (200 g) ground almonds

1⅔ cups (7 oz or 200 g) all-purpose flour

Sabayon:

8 egg yolks, **7** tbsps all-purpose flour

1¼ cups (9 oz or 250 g) sugar

1 cup (250 ml) Moscato wine

3/4 cup (200 ml) Marsala wine

Glaze:

4½ oz (130 g) dark chocolate

1½ tbsps butter, **3** eggs

2 tbsps confectioners' sugar

Cake base:

1 sponge cake round (see p. 386)

Grand Marnier

Preheat the oven to 350°F (180°C or Gas Mark 4).
Make the biscuit: Cream the softened butter with the sugar. Add the ground almonds and the flour and stir to combine. Spread the batter in a 1/2 inch (2 cm) layer in 2 cake pans the same diameter as the sponge cake round. Bake for 20 minutes.
Meanwhile, make the sabayon: Beat the egg yolks with the sugar. Sift in the flour, whisking constantly. Whisk in the Moscato wine and then the Marsala. Cover with a clean kitchen towel and refrigerate.
Make the chocolate glaze: Melt the chocolate with the butter over a double boiler.
Beat the eggs with the confectioners' sugar and add the melted chocolate mixture.
Moisten the sponge cake round with the Grand Marnier. Place 1 biscuit round on a serving plate and top it with half of the sabayon. Cover with the sponge cake round and top with the remaining sabayon.
Place the remaining biscuit round on top of the cake and coat the whole cake with the chocolate glaze.

Preparation time **40 minutes**
Cooking time **20 minutes**
Level **difficult**

individual chocolate-almond cakes with orange oil

Ingredients for 4 servings

Cake:

2 eggs

1/2 cup (3½ oz or 100 g) sugar

1½ cups (5½ oz or 150 g) ground almonds

1/4 cup (60 ml) Amaretto liqueur

5½ oz (150 g) dark chocolate

4 tbsps (2 oz or 50 g) butter

1 tsp baking powder

1 tsp vanilla extract

5 drops essential orange oil

1 tbsp cornstarch

Decoration:

confectioners' sugar

Preheat the oven to 350°F (180°C or Gas Mark 4).
Beat the eggs and sugar until thick and creamy.
Add the ground almonds and Amaretto liqueur and stir until smooth.
Melt the chocolate and butter over a double boiler.
Whisk into the egg mixture. Add the baking powder, vanilla, orange oil and cornstarch. Mix until smooth.
Butter and flour 4 small ramequins.
Pour the batter into the ramequins. Bake for 50 minutes.
Remove from oven and dust with confectioners' sugar.

Essential orange oil can also be used to flavor ice creams, cocktails and non-alcoholic drinks.

Preparation time **20 minutes**
Cooking time **55 minutes**
Level **easy**

spicy chocolate cake

Ingredients for 8 servings

Cake:

4 oz (110 g) chile-flavored dark chocolate, chopped

8 tbsps (4 oz or 110 g) butter, softened

1/2 cup (4 oz or 110 g) raw cane sugar

1/2 cup (4 oz or 110 g) all-purpose flour

3 eggs, separated

2 tbsps golden rum

2 oz (60 g) graham crackers, crumbled
salt

Decoration:

whipped cream or Chantilly cream

fresh chile peppers (optional)

The combination of chiles and chocolate has recently become fashionable, but it was first enjoyed by the ancient Aztecs and Mayans.

Preheat the oven to 350°F (180°C or Gas Mark 4).
Melt the chocolate over a double boiler or in the microwave. Cream the softened butter with the sugar until light and fluffy. Add the egg yolks one at a time and then pour in the melted chocolate. Mix well and add the rum.
Add the flour and crumble in the graham crackers.
Stir to combine.
Beat the egg whites and a pinch of salt to stiff peaks and fold them into the chocolate batter. Line a spring-form pan with parchment paper and pour in the batter.
Bake for 30 minutes. Let the cake cool completely.
Serve with whipped cream or Chantilly cream and decorate with fresh chile peppers if desired.

Preparation time **20 minutes**
Cooking time **40 minutes**
Level **easy**

walnut-fig tart

Ingredients for 8 servings

Filling:

1¾ cups (400 ml) milk

3/4 cup (5½ oz or 150 g) sugar

grated zest of 1 organic orange

1/3 cup (80 ml) vin cotto
(see note on p. 186)

1 tbsp extra-virgin olive oil

1 tbsp anise liqueur, like Pastis

1/2 tsp ground cinnamon

1/2 tsp vanilla extract

10 oz (280 g) dried figs, finely chopped

1/3 cup plus 1 tbsp (2 oz or 50 g)
chopped walnuts

3½ oz (100 g) dark chocolate

Crust:

4¾ cups (1⅓ lb or 600 g)
all-purpose flour

1 cup (7 oz or 200 g) sugar, 3 eggs

6 tbsps extra-virgin olive oil

1 tsp baking powder

Preheat the oven to 350°F (180°C or Gas Mark 4).
Place the milk, sugar, orange zest, vin cotto, olive oil,
anise liqueur, cinnamon and vanilla into a large saucepan.
Bring to a boil and cook until the mixture thickens.
Remove from heat and add the figs and walnuts. Let cool
completely. Add the coarsely chopped chocolate and puree
the mixture in a food processor. Let sit for 15 minutes.
Meanwhile, mix together all of the ingredients
for the crust to form a smooth dough. Roll out the dough
into a thin sheet on a lightly floured work surface.
Lightly oil a tart pan and line it with the dough.
Cut off any excess dough and set it aside.
Pour in the filling and roll out the remaining pastry dough.
Cut the dough into strips with a fluted rolling pastry cutter
and use the strips to create a lattice over the top
of the tart. Bake for 1 hour. Serve the tart warm or cold.

Preparation time **50 minutes**

Cooking time **1 hour**

Level **medium**

hazelnut cake with cappuccino

Ingredients for 4 servings

Cake:

5 eggs

1 cup (7 oz or 200 g) sugar

4 cups (10½ oz or 300 g) ground hazelnuts

1/2 cup (120 ml) prepared espresso coffee

10½ oz (300 g) dark chocolate

7 tbsps (3½ oz or 100 g) butter

2 tsps baking powder

2 tsps vanilla extract

3 tbsps cornstarch

1/2 cup (120 ml) milk

Preheat the oven to 350°F (180°C or Gas Mark 4).
Mix the eggs, sugar, hazelnuts and half the espresso in a mixing bowl.
Melt the chocolate and butter over a double boiler.
Whisk the chocolate into the egg mixture.
Add the baking powder, vanilla and cornstarch.
Stir carefully to form a smooth batter.
Pour the batter into a buttered cake pan and bake for 50 minutes. Meanwhile, heat the milk and whisk it until thick and foamy, then whisk in the remaining espresso.
Serve the cake and cappuccino together.

The chocolate may be melted in the microwave, on medium power, stirring frequently.

Preparation time **15 minutes**
Cooking time **50 minutes**
Level **easy**

flourless chocolate torte

Ingredients for 6-8 servings

Flourless:

9 oz (250 g) dark chocolate (70% cocoa)

14 tbsps (7 oz or 200 g) butter

1 cup (3½ oz or 100 g) confectioners' sugar

4 eggs

Preheat the oven to 350°F (180°C or Gas Mark 4).
Break the chocolate into pieces and place them over a double boiler. Melt the chocolate over low heat and then add the butter, stirring constantly.
Add the confectioners' sugar and stir until smooth.
Add the eggs one by one and mix well.
Butter and flour a loaf pan and pour the batter into the pan. Bake for 25-30 minutes.
Let the cake cool and then invert it onto a serving plate.

Serve this cake, if desired, with crème anglais: Boil 2 cups (500 ml) milk with the grated zest of 1 orange. Remove from the heat. Beat 4 eggs and 2/3 cup (4 oz or 125 g) sugar until thick and creamy. Whisk in the hot milk and return to the stove. Cook the cream over low heat until thick. Strain the cream into a cold bowl.

Preparation time **15 minutes**
Cooking time **30 minutes**
Level **easy**

Cakes

44

dark chocolate tart
with almonds

Ingredients for 4 servings

Tart:

7 oz (200 g) graham crackers

2½ cups (600 ml) maple syrup

3½ oz (100 g) extra-dark chocolate

2 tsps white almond cream

1 tbsp rice milk

Decoration:

2/3 cup (2 oz or 60 g) sliced almonds

Preheat the oven to 350°F (180°C or Gas Mark 4).
Crumble the graham crackers into a food processor
and add the maple syrup and rice milk.
Pulse the mixture until it comes together.
Line a cake pan with parchment paper and spread
in the batter in a thin layer.
Bake for 8 minutes, then let cool.
Melt the chocolate over a double boiler and add
the almond cream. Remove from the heat. When cooled
but still warm, spread the chocolate sauce over the tart.
Toast the sliced almonds in the oven for a few minutes
and then sprinkle them over the top of the tart.
Refrigerate for 1 hour and serve.

Acacia honey may be used
in place of the maple
syrup if desired.

Preparation time **15 minutes**
Cooking time **8 minutes**
Level **easy**

theresa's chocolate cake

Ingredients for 4 servings

Cake:

7 oz (200 g) dark chocolate

7 tbsps (3½ oz or 100 g) butter

3 eggs, separated

1/2 cup (3½ oz or 100 g) sugar

2 tbsps all-purpose flour

Preheat the oven to 350°F (180°C or Gas Mark 4).
Melt the chocolate and butter over a double boiler.
Meanwhile, beat the egg yolks and sugar until thick.
Carefully stir in the melted chocolate mixture
and add the flour. Beat the egg whites to stiff peaks and
fold them into the batter. Butter and flour a cake pan.
Pour the batter into the prepared pan and bake
for 50 minutes.
Let the cake cool and serve, if desired, sprinkled with
confectioners' sugar.

This simple chocolate cake is
delicious on its own or
accompanied by whipped
cream or orange marmalade.

Preparation time **30 minutes**
Cooking time **50 minutes**
Level **easy**

glazed chocolate-almond torte

Ingredients for 8 servings

Cake:

10½ oz (300 g) dark chocolate

1 cup (9 oz or 250 g) butter

5 eggs

4 tbsps sugar

1 cup (3½ oz or 100 g) ground almonds

1¼ cups (5½ oz or 150 g) all-purpose flour

1 tsp baking powder

Glaze:

4½ oz (125 g) dark chocolate

1/2 cup (120 ml) whipping cream

For a richer glaze, boil 3 tablespoons water with 3 tablespoons sugar. After 1 minute, pour in 3 tablespoons cream. Return to a boil and add 2½ oz (70 g) dark chocolate.

Preheat the oven to 320°F (160°C or Gas Mark 3).
Melt the chocolate and the butter in a saucepan until smooth. Let cool.
Beat the eggs with the sugar until foamy. Add the ground almonds, flour, baking powder and the melted chocolate.
Butter and flour a spring-form pan and pour in the batter.
Bake for 45 minutes.
Let the cake cool in the pan and then unmold. Heat the chocolate and cream in a saucepan over low heat.
Stir until melted and smooth.
Pour the glaze over the cake and serve.

Preparation time **15 minutes**
Cooking time **45 minutes**
Level **easy**

chocolate-almond tart

Ingredients for 6 servings
Crust:
1⅔ cups (7 oz or 200 g)
all-purpose flour
1/4 cup (2 oz or 50 g) sugar
8 tbsps (4 oz or 120 g) butter, cold
2 egg yolks, **1** tsp baking powder
Filling:
7 oz (200 g) dark chocolate
1/2 cup (100 ml) milk
1/3 cup (2½ oz or 75 g) sugar
3-4 graham crackers, crushed
1/4 cup (1 oz or 30 g) almonds,
coarsely chopped

The graham crackers can be replaced with amaretto cookies; their sweet flavor and fragrance pairs well with the almonds.

Preheat the oven to 320°F (160°C or Gas Mark 3).
Place the flour and sugar into a bowl and quickly cut in the cold butter. When the mixture resembles a coarse meal, add the egg yolks and baking powder and mix to form a compact dough.
Roll out the dough into a thin sheet.
Line a 10½-inch (26 cm) round tart tin with the dough, making a slightly thicker layer around the border.
Refrigerate the crust for 30 minutes.
Meanwhile, melt the chocolate with the milk over a double boiler. Add the sugar and mix well to incorporate.
Pour the chocolate mixture into the pastry crust and sprinkle with the crushed graham crackers and chopped almonds.
Bake the tart for 30 minutes. Remove from the oven, cool completely and cut into squares.

Preparation time **15 minutes**
Cooking time **40 minutes**
Level **easy**

marble cake

Ingredients for 6 servings

Cake:

4 cups (1 lb 2 oz or 500 g)
all-purpose flour

3 eggs

3/4 cup (5½ oz or 150 g) sugar

1/4 cup (60 ml) anise liqueur

1 cup (250 ml) milk

2 tsps baking powder

3/4 cup (6 oz or 170 g) butter
grated zest from 1/2 organic lemon

1/4 cup (1 oz or 25 g) cocoa powder

Preheat the oven to 350°F (180°C or Gas Mark 4).
Place the flour in a large mixing bowl.
Make a well in the center.
Add the eggs, sugar, anise liqueur, milk, 1/2 cup plus
2½ tbsps (5½ oz or 150 g) butter, baking powder and
the lemon zest in the center of the well.
Mix well to form a smooth batter. Pour 1/3 of the batter
into a smaller bowl and mix in the cocoa powder.
Butter and flour a cake pan and pour in half of the plain
batter. Top with the cocoa batter and then pour over
the remaining plain batter.
Bake until the cake is golden-brown on top,
about 30 minutes. Cool and serve.

To verify that the cake is done, insert a
toothpick into the center of the cake.
If the toothpick comes out clean, the
cake is done. However, if there is batter
or crumbs sticking to the toothpick the
cake needs to bake a little longer.

Preparation time **20 minutes**
Cooking time **30 minutes**
Level **easy**

almond tart with chocolate chips

Ingredients for 6 servings

Pastry:

1⅓ lb (600 g) shortcrust dough (see p. 386)

Filling:

1¾ cups (250 g) blanched almonds

13 tbsps (6½ oz or 180 g) butter

3/4 cup (5½ oz or 150 g) sugar cocoa powder

Decoration:

chocolate chips, butter

1 cup (250 ml) dry Marsala wine

Preheat the oven to 350°F (180°C or Gas Mark 4).
Roll out the dough on a lightly floured work surface,
reserving a small amount. Line a tart tin with the dough.
Sprinkle the cocoa powder over the dough.
Grind the almonds and place them in a warm oven
to remove any moisture. Transfer the almonds to a mixing
bowl and add the butter and sugar. Mix well.
Spread the mixture on a baking sheet and bake
for 10 minutes, or until golden-brown. Let cool.
Place the baked filling in the crust and top with
the chocolate chips and a few pat of butter.
Roll out the remaining pastry and cut it into strips.
Make a lattice top for the tart.
Bake for about 30 minutes.
Remove the tart from the oven and let cool slightly.
Brush the cake with the Marsala and cool completely.

Almonds have been used for centuries in pastry-making. Historical documents show that almonds were used to make primitive sweets prepared with honey, milk and fresh fruit and nuts.

Preparation time **20 minutes**
Cooking time **40 minutes**
Level **medium**

chocolate-almond torte

Ingredients for 6 servings

Torte:

3½ oz (100 g) dark chocolate

7 tbsps (3½ oz or 100 g) butter

2/3 cup (4 oz or 120 g) sugar

1½ cups (5 oz or 140 g) ground almonds

3 eggs, separated

1 tbsp breadcrumbs

Decoration:

confectioners' sugar

Preheat the oven to 350°F (180°C or Gas Mark 4).
Melt the chocolate in a saucepan over low heat.
Add the butter, sugar and ground almonds.
Remove from heat and let cool.
When cool, stir in the egg yolks. Beat the egg whites to stiff peaks and fold into the chocolate mixture.
Butter a tart tin and coat with breadcrumbs.
Pour the batter into the tart tin and bake for 35 minutes.
Remove the tart from the oven, let cool and dust with confectioners' sugar.

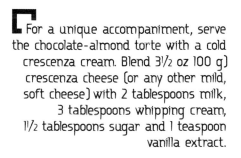

For a unique accompaniment, serve the chocolate-almond torte with a cold crescenza cream. Blend 3½ oz 100 g) crescenza cheese (or any other mild, soft cheese) with 2 tablespoons milk, 3 tablespoons whipping cream, 1½ tablespoons sugar and 1 teaspoon vanilla extract.

Preparation time **10 minutes**
Cooking time **35 minutes**
Level **easy**

apple cake with chocolate chips

Ingredients for 4 servings

Cake:

1/2 cup (4½ oz or 125 g) plain yogurt

2 eggs

7 tbsps corn oil

1/2 cup (3½ oz or 100 g)
raw cane sugar

1⅔ cups (7 oz or 200 g)
all-purpose flour

1/2 cup (3 oz or 80 g) chocolate chips

2 apples

1 tsp baking powder

1 pat of butter

Preheat the oven to 350°F (180°C or Gas Mark 4).
In a large bowl, mix the yogurt, eggs, corn oil, sugar,
flour and chocolate chips. Peel, core and dice the apples.
Add them to the batter and sprinkle over the baking
powder. Stir to combine. Butter and flour a cake pan.
Pour the batter into the prepared pan and bake
for 40-45 minutes.
Let cool slightly and serve.

This cake may be prepared 1 day in
advance. If desired, add a little
cinnamon to the batter.

Preparation time **10 minutes**
Cooking time **40 minutes**
Level **easy**

chocolate-peach cake

Ingredients for 4 servings

Cake:

5 eggs, **2** tbsps cocoa powder

1/3 cup plus **1** tbsp (3 oz or 80 g) raw cane sugar

2⅓ cups plus **1** tbsp (10½ oz or 300 g) all-purpose flour

3/4 cup (3½ oz or 100 g) cornstarch

7 tbsps (3½ oz or 100 g) butter, melted

1 tsp baking powder

1/2 tsp vanilla extract

Filling:

2/3 cup (7 oz or 200 g) peach jam

Frosting:

3½ oz (100 g) dark chocolate

2 tbsps whipping cream

 In the summer, substitute the peach jam with fresh peaches that have been marinated in lemon or orange juice and a few tablespoons of Cointreau.

Preheat the oven to 350°F (180°C or Gas Mark 4).
Beat the eggs with the sugar and add the flour, cornstarch and the melted butter. Sift in the cocoa powder and stir delicately until the cocoa is completely incorporated.
Add the baking powder and vanilla to the batter.
Butter and flour a cake pan and pour in the batter.
Bake for 35-40 minutes. Let cool completely.
Invert the cake onto a wire rack.
Slice in half horizontally. Spread the bottom half with the peach jam and cover with the top half.
Melt the chocolate and the cream over a double boiler.
Let cool slightly and spread over the cake in an even layer.
Refrigerate before serving.

Preparation time **25 minutes**
Cooking time **45 minutes**
Level **easy**

62

almond brownies

Ingredients for 6 servings

Brownies:

2 cups plus 1 tbsp (10½ oz or 300 g) almonds

3½ oz (100 g) dark chocolate

6 eggs, separated

1½ cups (10½ oz or 300 g) sugar

14 tbsps (7 oz or 200 g) butter

7 tsps cocoa powder

Decoration:

confectioners' sugar

Preheat the oven to 350°F (180°C or Gas Mark 4).
Chop the almonds and the chocolate together.
Beat the egg yolks with the sugar and mix in the butter and cocoa powder.
Beat the egg whites until they form stiff peaks and fold them into the batter. Pour the batter into a high-rimmed baking pan and bake for 40 minutes.
Invert the pan onto a wire rack and cut the brownies into squares. Sprinkle with confectioners' sugar and serve.

Serve the brownies with this light crème anglais: Heat 2 cups (500 ml) milk with half a vanilla bean. Beat 4 egg yolks with 2/3 cup (4 oz or 125 g) sugar. Whisk the hot milk into the egg mixture. When the cream has cooled, fold in 1/2 cup (120 ml) of whipped cream.

Preparation time **20 minutes**
Cooking time **40 minutes**
Level **easy**

glazed chocolate hearts

Ingredients for 4 servings
Cake:

7 oz (200 g) gianduia chocolate

5 eggs, separated

1/2 cup (3½ oz or 100 g) sugar

1/3 cup (2 oz or 50 g) toasted
almonds, chopped

1 oz (30 g) candied orange
peel, chopped

1/3 cup (1½ oz or 40 g)
all-purpose flour

salt, **1** pat of butter

Glaze:

7 oz (200 g) dark chocolate couverture

3 tbsps butter

Preheat the oven to 320°F (160°C or Gas Mark 3).
Melt the gianduia chocolate over a double boiler.
Beat the egg yolks with the sugar until creamy.
Whisk in the melted chocolate.
Add the almonds, candied orange and flour and mix well.
Beat the egg whites and a pinch of salt to stiff peaks.
Carefully fold into the chocolate mixture using a wooden
spoon. Butter and flour a 8½-inch (22 cm) spring-form
pan. Pour in the batter and bake for 30 minutes.
Remove the cake from the oven and cool slightly.
Invert the cake onto a work surface.
Cut out 4 hearts using a cookie cutter or a stencil.
Melt the couverture and butter together and pour
the glaze over the 4 cakes.
Let cool completely before serving.

To replace the couverture, use the
same quantity of dark chocolate and
add 3 tablespoons heavy cream.

Preparation time **25 minutes**
Cooking time **30 minutes**
Level **medium**

ricotta tart with chocolate

Ingredients for 6 servings

Crust:

2⅓ cups plus 1 tbsp (300 g) all-purpose flour

3 egg yolks

1/2 cup (3½ oz or 100 g) sugar, salt grated zest of 1 organic lemon

14 tbsps (7 oz or 200 g) butter, softened

Filling:

1 lb plus 2 tbsps (500 g) ricotta

3½ oz (100 g) candied pumpkin, diced

3½ oz (100 g) dark chocolate, finely chopped

1 cup (7 oz or 200 g) sugar

4 egg whites, **1** egg yolk

For a lighter pastry crust, substitute 3½ tbsps (2 oz or 50 g) butter with 1 teaspoon baking powder.

Preheat the oven to 350°F (180°C or Gas Mark 4).
Mix the flour with the 3 egg yolks, sugar, a pinch of salt, a little lemon zest and the softened butter.
Mix the ingredients well to form a smooth and soft dough.
Cover with a clean kitchen towel and let rest.
Meanwhile, sieve the ricotta into a mixing bowl.
Add the candied pumpkin, chocolate and sugar.
Beat the egg whites to stiff peaks and fold them into the ricotta mixture.
Divide the pastry dough in half and roll each half out into a thin sheet. Butter and flour a tart pan and line it with 1 sheet of pastry dough. Pour the ricotta filling into the tart crust. Top the tart with the remaining pastry sheet. Beat the remaining egg yolk and brush it over the top of the tart. Bake for 25 minutes.
Let cool and serve.

Preparation time **40 minutes**
Cooking time **25 minutes**
Level **easy**

chestnut tart with dark chocolate

Ingredients for 8 servings

Filling:

1¾ lb (800 g) chestnuts

10 fl oz (300 ml) milk

1/2 cup (3½ oz or 100 g) sugar

9 oz (250 g) dark chocolate, chopped

4 tbsps mascarpone

Crust:

2¾ cups (12½ oz or 350 g) all-purpose flour

1 egg

4 tbsps (3 oz or 80 g) butter, softened

3/4 cup (5½ oz or 150 g) sugar

1 tsp vanilla extract

1 bustina di vanillina

To peel chestnuts, remove the thick outer shell and soak overnight in a bowl of tepid, salted water. The thin skin that surrounds the chestnut will come away easily.

Preheat the oven to 350°F (180°C or Gas Mark 4).
Boil the chestnuts until soft.
Drain, peel and mash with a potato ricer.
Mix the mashed chestnut with the milk and sugar in a saucepan and cook for 10 minutes.
Add the chocolate and cook for another 10 minutes.
Add mascarpone and cook for 2 more minutes.
Remove from heat and let cool.
Mound the flour on a work surface and make a well in the center. Add the egg, softened butter, sugar and vanilla. Mix to form an elastic dough. If the dough seems to dry add a few teaspoons of warm water.
Divide the dough in half. Roll out half the dough into a sheet and place in a pie dish. Fill with chestnut cream and roll out the remaining dough. Cover the filling with the second sheet of dough; tuck the top sheet over the filling and fold the edges of the bottom sheet over to seal. Prick the top of the tart with a fork and bake for 45 minutes.
Remove from the oven and let cool.

Preparation time **30 minutes**
Cooking time **3 hours**
Level **easy**

walnut tart with chocolate glaze

Ingredients for 4 servings

Crust:

2⅓ cups plus 1 tbsp (10½ oz or 300 g) all-purpose flour

10 tbsps (5½ oz or 150 g) butter

7 tbsps (3½ oz or 100 g) sugar

3 egg yolks

grated zest of 1 organic lemon, salt

Filling:

2⅓ cups plus 1 tbsp (10½ oz or 300 g) chopped walnuts

3/4 cup (9 oz or 250 g) acacia honey

1 tbsp rum

Glaze:

3½ oz (100 g) dark chocolate, finely chopped

1/2 cup (3½ oz or 100 g) sugar

1 tbsp lemon juice

A round bottomed copper bowl or pot is useful for sauces and glazes that need to be cooked over a double boiler.

Preheat the oven to 350°F (180°C or Gas Mark 4).
Mix the flour, butter, sugar, egg yolks, lemon zest and salt to form a smooth dough.
Shape the dough into a ball and let rest for 30 minutes.
Divide the dough in half and roll it out into two rounds, one slightly larger than the other.
Butter a tart pan and line it with the larger of the two pastry rounds.
Grind the chopped walnuts in a food processor, transfer to a bowl and pour over the honey and rum.
Mix well and pour the mixture into the pastry crust.
Cover with the remaining pastry sheet and pinch the edges to seal. Bake for 35 minutes.
Meanwhile, prepare the glaze. Melt the chocolate over a double boiler over low heat. Place the sugar in a round-bottomed copper bowl or pot. Add a few drops of lemon juice and cook over a pan of simmering water until the mixture forms a ball. Whisk the sugar mixture into the melted chocolate stirring constantly.
Pour the hot glaze over the tart and smooth with a spatula. Serve immediately.

Preparation time **40 minutes**
Cooking time **1 hour**
Level **medium**

pastry roses with chocolate cream

Ingredients for 4 servings

Chocolate cream:

4 egg yolks, **2** cups (500 ml) milk

2/3 cup (4½ oz or 125 g) sugar

1/3 cup plus 1 tbsp (2 oz or 50 g) all-purpose flour

6½ oz (180 g) dark chocolate, chopped

Pastry:

3 tbsps (1½ oz or 40 g) butter

3/4 cup (3 oz or 90 g) confectioners' sugar

2 eggs, **1** tsp vanilla extract, salt

1⅔ cups (7½ oz or 210 g) all-purpose flour

4 tbsps milk, **1** tbsp malt extract

Cakes

74

For a sweet variation, try substituting the dark chocolate with the same quantity of milk chocolate and a few finely chopped amaretto cookies.

Preheat the oven to 350°F (180°C or Gas Mark 4).
Make the cream: Beat the egg yolks with the sugar using an electric beater. Sift in the flour and mix until smooth. Heat the milk to a boil and whisk it into the egg mixture. Return to heat and cook over medium heat, stirring constantly, until the cream thickens.
Add the chocolate to the cream, stirring until the chocolate has melted.
Make the pastry: Cream the butter and sugar. Add the eggs, vanilla, a pinch of salt and the flour. Mix to form a smooth dough. Wrap in plastic wrap and let rest in the refrigerator.
Roll out the dough into a thin sheet and cut it into four 1½ -by-8-inch (4 by 20 cm) strips.
Transfer the chocolate cream to a pastry bag and pipe a line of chocolate cream onto each strip. Roll up the strips to form roses and place them on a baking sheet.
Heat the milk and malt extract over low heat.
Brush the roses with the milk mixture and bake until the edges begin to brown, about 10 minutes.
Serve, if desired, with crème anglais.

Preparation time **20 minutes**
Cooking time **15 minutes**
Level **medium**

caprese cake

Ingredients for 6 servings

Cake:

2 cups (10½ oz or 300 g) almonds

1 cup (7 oz or 200 g) sugar, **5** eggs

10 oz (280 g) dark chocolate

7 tbsps (3½ oz or 100 g) butter

1/4 cup (60 ml) Amaretto liqueur

1 tsp almond extract

2 tsps vanilla extract

3 tbsps cornstarch, salt

2 tsps baking powder

Decoration:

confectioners' sugar

Preheat the oven to 350°F (180°C or Gas Mark 4).
Blend the almonds in a food processor with the sugar
to the consistency of a coarse meal.
Transfer to a mixing bowl and stir in the eggs.
Melt the chocolate and butter together and let cool
slightly. Add the Amaretto liqueur, vanilla and almond
extracts, cornstarch and a pinch of salt to the egg mixture.
Add the chocolate to the egg mixture and stir to combine.
Sift in the baking powder and mix to incorporate.
Butter and flour the sides of a 9-inch (22 cm) spring-form
pan. Cut out a 9-inch (22 cm) round of parchment paper
and line the bottom of the pan.
Pour the cake batter into the pan and bake for 45 minutes.
Sprinkle the cake with confectioners' sugar
and serve warm.

Preparation time **20 minutes**
Cooking time **55 minutes**
Level **easy**

Cakes

dark chocolate desserts

chocolate

strawberries on brioche with crème anglais

Ingredients for 4 servings
Crème Anglais:

1 basket of strawberries, hulled and diced

1 tbsp sugar

2 mint leaves, finely chopped

4 slices brioche bread

3½ oz (100 g) dark chocolate

2 cups (500 ml) milk grated zest of 1 lemon

4 egg yolks

2/3 cup (4½ oz or 125 g) sugar

1 tsp cornstarch

1 tbsp whipping cream

Mix the strawberries, sugar and mint leaves together and let sit. Cut the brioche slices into 4 rounds and toast them slightly.

Melt the chocolate over a double boiler and dip the toasted bread in the chocolate. Set the chocolate-coated bread on a sheet of waxed paper and let harden.

Heat the milk and lemon zest together. Beat the egg yolks and sugar with the cornstarch. Whisk the hot milk into the eggs and then transfer the mixture back to the saucepan.

Cook the cream over low heat until it coats the back of a wooden spoon. Place the saucepan in a cold water bath and let the cream cool completely.

Place the chocolate-covered brioche on individual serving plates. Place a round cookie cutter on the bread and fill with the strawberry mixture. Carefully remove the cookie cutter so that the strawberries hold their shape.

Top with cold crème anglais and a little whipped cream.

Cookie cutters are usually made of stainless steel or plastic and come in many sizes and shapes.

Preparation time **25 minutes**
Cooking time **20 minutes**
Level **easy**

spiced hot chocolate

Ingredients for 4 servings
Spiced:

7 tbsps milk

1 tbsp sugar

1 dried red chili pepper

1 cinnamon stick, broken into pieces

1 clove

7 tbsp whipping cream

3½ oz (100 g) extra-dark chocolate, chopped

Heat the milk together with the sugar, chili pepper, cinnamon and clove.
Let infuse for 3-4 hours and then strain the mixture.
Heat the infused milk with the whipping cream.
Add the chocolate and let melt completely.
Let cool and serve in small glasses or ceramic cups.
This delicious drink can be served with chocolate-based desserts.

This hot chocolate may also be used as a sauce for ice cream.

Preparation time **25 minutes**
Cooking time **15 minutes**
Level **easy**

spicy chocolate frappé

Ingredients for 2 servings

Frappé:

7 tbsps milk

1/4 fresh red chili pepper, diced

7 oz (200 g) dark-chocolate ice cream

10 hazelnuts

Decoration:

slivered hazelnuts

Heat half of the milk with the chili pepper, then remove from the heat and let infuse for 1 hour.
Strain the milk, pour into an ice tray and freeze.
Once the infused milk is frozen, place the cubes in a blender with the chocolate ice cream.
Add the remaining milk and hazelnuts and blend until creamy. Pour into glasses and top with slivered hazelnuts.

 For a fizzy float: Place 2 scoops of hazelnut ice cream in glasses, pour over enough sparkling water to fill the glass half-full and mix well. Top with 1 scoop of chocolate ice cream and fill the glass with more sparkling water.

Preparation time **10 minutes**
Cooking time **2 minutes**
Level **easy**

pancakes with chocolate-cinnamon cream

Ingredients for 4 servings

Pancakes:

3/4 cup plus 1 tbsp (3½ oz or 100 g) self-rising flour

salt, **1** egg

3 tbsps sugar

1 tsp vanilla extract

2/3 cup (150 ml) milk

1 tbsp butter

Cream:

5½ oz (150 g) extra-dark cinnamon-flavored chocolate

3 tbsps whipping cream

Place the flour into a mixing bowl with a pinch of salt.
Mix in the egg, sugar and vanilla and whisk in the milk.
Stir vigorously to obtain a smooth batter.
Let rest for 20 minutes in a cool place.
Chop the chocolate and melt it over a double boiler with the cream, stirring frequently.
When the sauce is smooth, remove from the heat.
Cool until the sauce becomes creamy.
Heat a non-stick pan or griddle. Melt the butter and when it sizzles, add 1 spoonful of batter.
Let it cook for about 3 minutes, until the bubbles that form on the surface begin to pop.
Flip the pancake and cook for another 2 minutes.
Continue making pancakes until the batter is finished.
Layer the pancakes with the chocolate-cinnamon cream and serve.

86

If cinnamon-flavored chocolate is not available, use plain chocolate and add a pinch of ground cinnamon to the chocolate cream.

Preparation time **30 minutes**
Cooking time **25 minutes**
Level **easy**

chocolate-pumpkin soufflés

Ingredients for 4 servings

Soufflés:

4 large eggs, separated

1/2 cup (3½ oz or 100 g) raw cane sugar

1 tbsp all-purpose flour

1/2 tsp vanilla extract, salt

5 tbsps cocoa powder

7 tbsps (3½ oz or 100 g) melted butter

1/2 cup (2 oz or 60 g) diced pumpkin or other winter squash

Sauce:

2 oz (60 g) extra-dark chocolate

2 tbsps whipping cream

The name soufflé derives from the French verb souffler, to blow. Soufflés can be sweet or savory and are all made using the same basic technique which uses the egg yolks as a base and whites as a lightening and rising agent.

Preheat the oven to 350°F (180°C or Gas Mark 4).
Bake the pumpkin for 25 minutes.
Meanwhile, beat the egg yolks until they are thick and pale yellow in color.
Add the sugar, flour, vanilla and a pinch of salt.
Mix well and add the cocoa powder and melted butter.
Mash or puree the cooked pumpkin and stir into the batter.
Preheat the oven to 400°F (200°C or Gas Mark 6).
Beat the egg whites and a pinch of salt to stiff peaks.
Fold them into the soufflé batter.
Butter 4 ramequins and sprinkle them with sugar.
Pour the batter into the ramequins and bake for 20-25 minutes.
Meanwhile, melt the chocolate and whipping cream over a double boiler. Serve the soufflés with the chocolate sauce as soon as they come out of the oven.

Preparation time **10 minutes**
Cooking time **25 minutes**
Level **easy**

mocha panna cotta

Ingredients for 8 servings
Panna Cotta:

3/4 cup plus 1 tbsp (200 ml) milk

3/4 cup plus 1 tbsp (200 ml) whipping cream

3 tbsps sugar

2 gelatin sheets

1/4 cup (60 ml) sweetened espresso coffee

7 oz (200 g) dark chocolate, finely chopped

Bring the milk, cream and sugar to a boil in a saucepan. Soak the gelatin in cold water for a few minutes, drain and squeeze out excess water. Add the gelatin and espresso to the milk mixture. Mix well and let cool slightly. Whisk the chocolate into the warm cream mixture. Stir until the chocolate melts. Pour the mixture into 8 ramequins lined with plastic wrap. Refrigerate for 3 hours. Unmold the panna cottas and serve.

For a thicker consistency, substitute the milk with the same quantity of whipping cream.

Preparation time **20 minutes**
Cooking time **10 minutes**
Level **easy**

vanilla puddings with chocolate sauce

Ingredients for 4 servings
Vanilla Puddings:

2/3 cup (150 ml) milk

1 vanilla bean, halved lengthwise grated zest of 1 lime, **1** egg yolk

1/3 cup (2 oz or 60 g) sugar

2 gelatin sheets

2/3 cup (150 ml) whipping cream

Chocolate sauce:

3 tbsps (50 ml) whipping cream

3½ oz (100 g) clove-flavored dark chocolate, chopped

Decoration:

4 cape gooseberries, cocoa powder

Bring the milk to a boil with the vanilla bean and lime zest. Strain the milk and return to the pan.
Beat the egg yolk with the sugar and whisk in the hot milk. Soak the gelatin in a little cold water, drain and squeeze out the excess liquid. Dissolve the gelatin in the milk and egg mixture and let cool.
Beat the cream to stiff peaks and fold it into the milk mixture.Pour the batter into 4 conical molds.
Refrigerate for 2 hours.
Make the sauce: Heat the cream in a saucepan. Add the chocolate to the cream, stirring until it melts completely. Unmold the vanilla puddings and place them on individual serving plates.
Decorate the plates with the cape gooseberries and cocoa powder. Drizzle the chocolate sauce over the vanilla puddings and serve.

Desserts

92

Cape gooseberries, also known as physallis, are beautiful orange berries surrounded by papery petals, which look like miniature Chinese lanterns. They may be used fresh, candied or covered with chocolate.

Preparation time **30 minutes**
Cooking time **20 minutes**
Level **medium**

ricotta and panettone pudding

Ingredients for 4 servings

Pudding:

2 eggs, separated

1/2 cup (4 oz or 110 g) sugar

1/4 cup (1 oz or 30 g) all-purpose flour, sifted

2/3 cup (150 ml) milk

4 oz (120 g) panettone, diced

3½ oz (100 g) ricotta
hazelnut chocolate, shaved

Beat the egg yolks with the sugar and add the sifted flour.
Bring the milk to a boil in a saucepan.
Whisk the milk into the eggs and then return the mixture to the saucepan. Cook the cream over low heat, stirring constantly until the cream thickens.
Pour the pastry cream into a bowl and let cool slightly.
Meanwhile, cut the panettone into small pieces and add them to the pastry cream.
When the mixture has cooled completely stir in the ricotta.
Mix well and refrigerate for 1 hour.
Top with shavings of hazelnut chocolate before serving.

To make a more chocolatey version of this dessert, add 2½ oz (70 g) of shaved chocolate to the pastry cream while it is cooking. Stir well to melt the chocolate completely, or remove the cream from the heat immediately to retain a variegated (stracciatella) effect.

Preparation time **20 minutes**
Cooking time **15 minutes**
Level **easy**

apple mousse in chocolate rings

Ingredients for 4 servings

Chocolate rings:

1½ oz (40 g) dark chocolate

Sponge cake:

4 small rounds of sponge cake (see p. 386)

Apple mousse:

2 gelatin sheets, **2** eggs

3 tbsps (2 oz or 50 g) sugar

1/3 cup plus 2 tbsps (3 oz or 100 g) applesauce

9 tbsps (4½ oz or 125 g) butter, at room temperature

Vanilla sauce:

3/4 cup plus 1 tbsp (210 ml) whipping cream

1/2 vanilla bean, **2** eggs

1/3 cup (2 oz or 60 g) sugar

Decoration:

mint leaves

Melt the chocolate and spread it into 2-by-10-inch (4 by 25 cm) rectangles onto a Silpat, making a total of 4 rectangles. Before the chocolate hardens completely, use each one to line a 3-inch (7½ cm) round cookie cutter. Refrigerate the chocolate rings until hardened. Remove the rings from the refrigerator and unmold the chocolate. Trim the sponge cake rounds to the same size, and place a round in the bottom of each chocolate ring. Place a spoonful of applesauce in the bottom of each ring. Return to the refrigerator. Make the mousse: soak the gelatin in cold water for a few minutes. Beat the eggs with the sugar and heat the remaining applesauce. Drain the gelatin, squeeze out the excess water and add it to the warm applesauce. Pour the applesauce into an electric mixer and add the butter. Beat to combine. Add the egg mixture to the apple-butter emulsification and mix. Fill the chocolate rings with the apple mousse and refrigerate for 3 hours. Make the sauce: Beat the eggs with the sugar. Bring the whipping cream to a boil with the vanilla bean. Remove the vanilla bean and whisk the hot cream into the egg mixture. Return to the saucepan and cook, stirring until the cream coats the back of a spoon. Place the chocolate rings on individual plates and top with the vanilla sauce. Decorate with mint leaves and serve.

Preparation time **1 hour**
Cooking time **15 minutes**
Level **difficult**

chocolate, coffee and almond trifle

Ingredients for 6 servings
Trifle:

6 egg yolks, **2** gelatin sheets
10 tbsps (5½ oz or 150 g) butter
1 cup plus 1 tbsp (5 oz or 140 g)
confectioner's sugar
3/4 cup (200 ml) Marsala wine
1/2 cup (100 ml) whipping cream
3½ oz (100 g) dark chocolate, chopped
3 tbsps cold espresso coffee
2/3 cup (3½ oz or 100 g) almonds,
toasted and chopped
7 oz (200 g) amaretto cookies
7 oz (200 g) ladyfingers
Decoration:
dark chocolate shavings

It is believed that amaretto cookies were invented in Venice during the Renaissance. Today the cookies are widely used in Italian cuisine. Various types of amaretto cookies are available: soft, hard and sugar-coated.

Beat the egg yolks, butter and confectioner's sugar into a soft cream. Bring 1/2 of the Marsala wine to a boil and whisk it into the egg mixture. Soak the gelatin in cold water, drain, squeeze out the excess liquid and add it to the egg mixture. Whip the whipping cream to stiff peaks and fold it into the egg mixture. Divide the cream evenly between 2 small bowls and 1 large mixing bowl. Add the chopped chocolate to one of the small bowls and stir to combine. Gradually whisk the coffee into the second small bowl. Add the almonds to the large bowl.
Slice the ladyfingers in half and brush them with some of the remaining Marsala. Lightly press them down and place half of them in a round on the serving plate. Pour the chocolate cream over the ladyfingers and smooth to cover completely. Brush the amaretto cookies with Marsala and place them on top of the chocolate cream. Pour the coffee cream over the amaretto cookies and smooth to cover. Top with the remaining ladyfingers. Pour over the almond cream, smooth with a spatula and refrigerate for 3 hours.
Serve cold decorated with chocolate shavings.

Preparation time **30 minutes**
Cooking time **10 minutes**
Level **medium**

dark-chocolate mousse
with strawberries

Ingredients for 4 servings

Mousse:

9 oz (250 g) dark chocolate

2/3 cup (150 ml) whipping cream

2 gelatin sheets

5 tbsps white rum

2 egg whites

salt

2 tbsps sugar

Decoration:

2 small baskets of strawberries, hulled and sliced

Melt the chocolate over a double boiler. Remove from heat and let cool.
Whip the cream and fold it into the chocolate.
Soak the gelatin in cold water. Drain and squeeze out the excess water. Add the gelatin and the rum to the chocolate mixture.
Beat the egg whites with a pinch of salt until foamy. Add the sugar and beat to stiff peaks. Fold the egg whites into the mousse.
Refrigerate for 4 hours and decorate with sliced strawberries.

Mousse is one of the many cooking terms that derives from French. It usually describes a soft light cream made with eggs, either sweet or savory.

Preparation time **15 minutes**
Cooking time **5 minutes**
Level **easy**

coconut and chocolate ganache desserts

Ingredients for 4 servings

Coconut:

1/2 coconut

Chocolate ganache:

7 oz (200 g) dark chocolate, chopped

1/2 cup (100 ml) whipping cream

1/3 cup (1½ oz or 40 g) ground hazelnuts

Decoration:

2 oz (50 g) amaretto cookies

Break the coconut half into several pieces and remove the meat from the shell. Finely chop the coconut meat. Melt the chocolate over a double boiler and add the whipping cream, stirring frequently to create a smooth cream. Place 4 round molds or ramequins on a tray. Layer the coconut, chocolate ganache and ground hazelnuts into the ramequins. Place the tray in the refrigerator and chill for at least 30 minutes. Top with crumbled amaretto cookies before serving.

For a richer alternative, mix 2 tablespoons of coconut liqueur into the chopped coconut before layering it into the ramequins. Top the coconut dessert with a drizzle of melted dark chocolate.

Preparation time **15 minutes**
Cooking time **15 minutes**
Level **easy**

chocolate soufflé
with basil sabayon

Ingredients for 4 servings
Soufflé:

9 oz (250 g) dark chocolate, chopped
6 eggs, separated, plus 1 egg white
1/2 cup (3½ oz or 100 g)
raw cane sugar
1 tsp vanilla extract
1/4 cup (1 oz or 25 g) cocoa powder
2½ tbsps cornstarch, salt
1 pat of butter, all-purpose flour

Sabayon:

3 egg yolks, **6** basil leaves, chopped
1/3 cup (2 oz or 60 g) sugar
2/3 cup (150 ml) whipping cream

Decoration:

seeds from 1 ripe pomegranate
1/2 papaya, peeled and diced

Preheat the oven to 350°F (180°C or Gas Mark 4).
Make the soufflé: Melt the chocolate over a double boiler.
Beat the egg yolks with the sugar and the vanilla.
Sift in the cocoa powder and cornstarch.
Add the chocolate and mix well.
Beat the egg whites and a pinch of salt to stiff peaks
and carefully fold them into the egg mixture.
Butter and flour 6 aluminum ramequins.
Fill the ramequins three-quarters-full with the soufflé
batter and bake for 30 minutes.
Cool the soufflés for at least 15 minutes.
Meanwhile, make the sabayon: Beat the egg yolks with
the sugar. Whisk in the whipping cream and chopped basil
leaves. Serve the soufflés with the sabayon on plates
decorated with pomegranate seeds and diced papaya.

Cane sugar was known as far back
as Roman times, however it has only
commonly been used for cooking
since the colonial period.

Preparation time **20 minutes**
Cooking time **30 minutes**
Level **medium**

almond cake with cinnamon gelato

Desserts

Ingredients for 8 servings

Almond cake:

6 eggs, separated, white chocolate

1½ cups (300 g) sugar

3½ oz (100 g) dark chocolate, chopped

3 cups (10½ oz or 300 g) ground almonds

14 tbsps (7 oz or 200 g) melted butter

7 tsps unsweetened cocoa powder

Gelato:

2 egg yolks, **1** tsp dextrose

1/3 cup (2½ oz or 70 g) sugar

1 cup plus 2 tbsps (270 ml) milk

3 tbsps whipping cream

4 cinnamon sticks, **1** tsp glucose syrup

1/4 cup (1 oz or 25 g) powdered milk

Dextrose or glucose syrups are available in specialty baking stores. Using glucose and dextrose improves the consistency of gelato.

Preheat the oven to 350°F (180°C or Gas Mark 4).
Make the cake: Beat the egg yolks and sugar until they are thick. Add the chocolate, almonds, butter and cocoa powder.
Beat the egg whites to stiff peaks and fold into the batter.
Pour the batter into cake pan and bake for 40 minutes.
Invert the cake onto a wire rack and let cool.
Melt the white chocolate and drizzle it over the cake.
Make the gelato: Beat the egg yolks, sugar and dextrose until thick and pale yellow.
Heat the milk, cream and glucose syrup in a saucepan. Whisk in the powdered milk. Break up the cinnamon sticks and add them to the milk mixture. When the milk begins to boil, remove from heat. Strain the milk mixture and whisk it into the egg yolk mixture. Return to heat and cook, stirring constantly, until it reaches 185°F (85°C). Cool quickly and pour into an ice-cream machine.
Follow the manufacturer's instructions to freeze the ice cream. Cut out 8 small rounds of cake and serve with the cinnamon gelato.

Preparation time **35 minutes**
Cooking time **1 hour**
Level **medium**

iced mocha soufflés

Ingredients for 4 servings

Soufflés:

2 oz (60 g) coffee-flavored dark chocolate

1/2 cup (125 ml) water

1/3 cup (1 oz or 30 g) cocoa powder

1/2 cup (3½ oz or 100 g) sugar

2 egg whites, salt

2 tbsps Grand Marnier

1½ cups (300 ml) whipping cream

Decoration:

instant coffee

sweetened cocoa powder

Melt the chocolate over a double boiler.
In another pan heat 4 tablespoons of water with the cocoa powder. In another small saucepan heat the sugar with the remaining water without stirring until it reaches 240°F (115°C).
Meanwhile beat the egg whites with a pinch of salt. When the whites become frothy slowly pour in the sugar syrup. Continue beating until the whites form stiff, shiny peaks. Fold in the melted chocolate and the cocoa powder mixture. Add the Grand Marnier and stir to combine.
Beat the whipping cream to stiff peaks and fold it into the batter. Make a parchment paper border around the top of 4 tea cups. Pour the batter into the tea cups and freeze for at least 2 hours.
Remove the paper, dust with instant coffee and cocoa powder and serve.

A candy thermometer is a useful kitchen tool which helps measure the temperature of the sugar syrup in this recipe. It can also be used to measure the temperature of oil when frying.

Preparation time **25 minutes**
Cooking time **10 minutes**
Level **medium**

chocolate zuccotto

Ingredients for 4 servings

Zuccotto:

2 sponge cake rounds (see p. 386)

3/4 cups plus 1 tbsp (200 ml) sweet liqueur or Vin Santo

2 cups (500 ml) whipping cream

1 cup (7 oz or 200 g) sugar

4 oz (120 g) dark chocolate

1/3 cup (1 oz or 30 g) cocoa powder

Decoration:

chocolate shavings (optional)

Cut the sponge cake into strips and line a bombe mold with the cake. Pour some of the sweet liqueur or Vin Santo over the sponge cake to moisten.
Shave the chocolate with a sharp knife.
Beat the whipping cream with the sugar and divide it between 2 bowls. Add the chocolate shavings to one of the bowls and stir to combine.
Add the cocoa powder to the second bowl.
Fill the zuccotto with alternating layers of the two creams. Moisten the second round of sponge cake with the remaining liqueur or Vin Santo and place it on top of the zuccotto. Cover with plastic wrap and freeze for 3-4 hours. Unmold and decorate, if desired, with chocolate shavings.

The name of this typical Italian dessert comes from the word zucca, meaning pumpkin, and refers to its rounded shape.

Preparation time **40 minutes**
Level **medium**

chocolate banana frappé

Ingredients for 4 servings
Frappé:

3/4 cup plus 1 tbsp (200 ml) rice milk

1/2 vanilla bean

3 oz (80 g) dark chocolate, chopped

1 ripe banana

Heat the rice milk with the vanilla bean. Remove from heat and let infuse for at least 10 minutes. Remove the vanilla bean and add the chopped chocolate. Stir the mixture over low heat until the chocolate is melted. Let cool completely.
Place the chocolate milk and the banana in a blender and blend until the mixture is thick and foamy.
Serve cold.

Desserts

Rice milk is low in fat and also relatively low in protein. It is a cereal-based drink that is often used in vegan or vegetarian cooking to replace cow's milk.

Preparation time **10 minutes**
Cooking time **5 minutes**
Level **easy**

chocolate honeycombs
with pineapple and orange sabayon

Ingredients for 4 servings
Honeycombs:

4 oz (120 g) dried pineapple
juice and grated zest
of 1 organic orange

7 oz (200 g) dark chocolate, chopped

1 egg yolk

2 tbsps (25 g) raw sugar

6 tbsps Barolo Chinato liqueur

ground cinnamon

Soak the dried pineapple in some water and the orange juice. Melt all but 2 tablespoons of the chopped chocolate over a double boiler.
Let cool slightly, then mix in the remaining chocolate while still warm. Cut a piece of bubble wrap packaging into four 2½ -by-4-inch (5 by 10 cm) strips.
Spread a layer of melted chocolate over each strip and when the chocolate begins to harden fold each strip into a cylinder so that the two ends meet. When cooled completely remove the bubble wrap and place the chocolate honeycombs on serving plates.
Drain the pineapple and cut it into little strips.
Fill the chocolate cups with the pineapple.
Beat the egg yolk in a round-bottomed sabayon bowl with the sugar, Barolo Chinato, cinnamon and orange zest.
Place the sabayon over a pan of simmering water and beat until the mixture becomes thick and foamy.
Remove from the heat and place a few spoonfuls of sabayon in each chocolate cup.

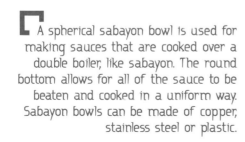 A spherical sabayon bowl is used for making sauces that are cooked over a double boiler, like sabayon. The round bottom allows for all of the sauce to be beaten and cooked in a uniform way. Sabayon bowls can be made of copper, stainless steel or plastic.

Preparation time **40 minutes**
Cooking time **10 minutes**
Level **difficult**

chocolate bavarian creams

Ingredients for 2 servings
Bavarian creams:
1 cup (250 ml) milk
grated zest of 1 orange
4 gelatin sheets
3 oz (80 g) dark chocolate, chopped
2 egg yolks
1/2 cup (3½ oz or 100 g) sugar
1 cup (250 ml) whipping cream
1/2 cup (125 ml) Grand Marnier
Decoration:
zest of 1 orange, julienned
dark chocolate shavings

Bring the milk to a boil with the orange zest.
Soak the gelatin sheets in cold water for a few minutes.
Drain and squeeze out the excess water.
Transfer half the hot milk to a bowl and dissolve
the chocolate in the milk. Beat the egg yolks and the
sugar together and add the chocolate and the milk.
Return to the saucepan and cook over low heat.
Add the gelatin and mix until the cream begins to thicken.
Remove from heat, sieve the mixture and let cool.
Whip the whipping cream and fold into the cooled
chocolate mixture.
Coat 4 ramequins with Grand Marnier. Pour the chocolate
cream into the ramequins and refrigerate for 3 hours.
Unmold the Bavarian creams and decorate with julienned
orange zest and shaved chocolate.

Bavarian cream is a classic dessert
that uses eggs, milk, cream and gelatin.
For a lighter version, replace the whipping
cream with 3 beaten egg whites.

Preparation time **25 minutes**
Cooking time **5 minutes**
Level **easy**

cocoa blinis withdark chocolate sauce

Ingredients for 6 servings
Blinis:

1 packet (2¼ tsp) active dry yeast

1¾ cups (400 ml) warm milk

2/3 cup (2 oz or 50 g) cocoa powder

2 cups (9 oz or 250 g) all-purpose flour

3/4 cup (3½ oz or 100 g) buckwheat flour

3 tbsps sugar, salt

2/3 cup (150 ml) whipping cream

3 eggs, separated

4 tbsps (2 oz or 60 g) butter

Chocolate sauce:

3½ oz (100 g) dark chocolate, chopped

2 tbsps whipping cream

Blinis are small pancakes that come from the Ukrainian culinary tradition. They are smaller in size and thicker than traditional pancakes as they are made with yeast.

Dissolve the yeast in 1 cup (250 ml) warm milk. Sift the cocoa powder and two flours into a bowl and add the sugar and salt.
Mix well and add the yeast mixture, remaining milk and cream. Add the egg yolks and stir to form a smooth batter. Cover and let rise for 1 hour.
Beat the egg whites and a pinch of salt to stiff peaks and fold them into the batter. Melt the butter and add it to the batter as well. Let rest for 30 minutes.
Melt a little butter in a non-stick frying pan.
Cook the blinis until golden brown. Meanwhile, melt the chocolate and cream together over a double boiler or in the microwave.
Serve the blinis hot, drizzled with the chocolate sauce.

Preparation time **20 minutes**
Cooking time **15 minutes**
Level **easy**

chocolate crème brûlée

Ingredients for 6 servings

Crème Brûlée:

3/4 cup plus 1 tbsp (200 ml) whipping cream

7 tbsps milk

2 egg yolks

3 tbsps sugar

1 tsp cornstarch

2 drops hazelnut extract

3 oz (80 g) extra-dark chocolate, chopped

1 tbsp raw cane sugar

Heat the cream and milk in a saucepan without boiling.
Beat the egg yolks and the sugar in a mixing bowl.
Add the cornstarch and hazelnut extract.
Slowly whisk the warm milk mixture into the eggs.
Transfer to a double boiler and make sure that the water never comes to a boil. Cook the cream until it coats the back of a spoon. Add the chopped chocolate and stir to combine. Remove from the heat and pour into 4 ceramic ramequins. Refrigerate until ready to serve.
Preheat the broiler.
Sprinkle the crème brûlées with the raw cane sugar and broil until the sugar caramelizes.
Serve immediately.

 If using the broiler to finish the crème brûlées, it is best to place the ramequins in a baking dish filled with cold water and broil until the sugar has caramelized. This way the heat from the grill will not overcook the crème brûlées.

Preparation time **25 minutes**
Cooking time **15 minutes**
Level **easy**

chocolate shells with vanilla cream and caramelized bananas

Ingredients for 4 servings
Chocolate shells:
7 oz (200 g) dark chocolate
Vanilla Sauce:
7 tbsps milk
1 vanilla bean, sliced lengthwise
3 tbsps whipping cream
1 tbsp confectioners' sugar
Caramelized bananas:
1 pat of butter
1 tbsp raw cane sugar
1 ripe banana, sliced
golden rum

Melt the chocolate and pour it into 4 shell-shaped molds.
Pour out any excess chocolate.
Let harden in a cool, dry place.
Bring the milk and vanilla to a boil and remove from heat.
Let infuse for 20 minutes. Strain the infusion.
Whip the cream just until it begins to form soft peaks.
Fold it into the vanilla infusion, add the confectioner's sugar and refrigerate.
Heat a tabof butter in a non-stick frying pan
and sprinkle the bottom of the pan with the raw cane sugar. When the sugar begins to caramelize add the banana and brown for 1 minute. Pour over the rum and let it evaporate. Remove from heat.
Fill the chocolate shells half-full with the vanilla sauce and top with the warm, caramelized bananas.

Ready-made chocolate bases are available in many shapes and sizes. Remember to choose a concave shape that will hold the sauce and bananas for this recipe.

Preparation time **30 minutes**
Cooking time **15 minutes**
Level **medium**

dark chocolate mousse with sweet cream foam and mandarin Sauce

Ingredients for 6 servings

Mousse:

9 oz (250 g) dark chocolate, chopped

1 gelatin sheet

2 egg whites

1 tbsp sugar, salt

2/3 cup (150 ml) whipping cream

5 tbsps dark rum

2 tbsps chopped pistachios

Foam:

4 tbsps sweetened condensed milk

3 tbsps whipping cream

1 egg white

Sauce:

1 pat of butter

raw cane sugar

2 mandarins, white rum

Melt the chocolate over a double boiler.
Soak the gelatin sheet in cold water for a few minutes.
Drain and squeeze out excess water.
Dissolve the gelatin in a small saucepan over low heat.
Whip the egg whites, sugar and a pinch of salt into
stiff peaks. Whip the whipping cream into stiff peaks.
Transfer the melted chocolate to a bowl, fold in the
whipped cream, then the gelatin, rum and finally the egg
whites. Refrigerate for 2 hours. Pour all of the ingredients
for the foam into a whipped cream canister (soda siphon),
close with the gas cartridge and refrigerate. Meanwhile,
peel the mandarins and separate the segments. Melt
the butter in a frying pan with the sugar. Add the mandarin
segments and let caramelize slightly. Add the white rum
and let evaporate. Add a little hot water and reduce
the sauce by half. Puree the sauce in a blender or food
processor, then pass through a sieve.
Spoon the mousse into 6 small bowls.
Drizzle with mandarin sauce and sprinkle with pistachios.
Use the whipped cream canister to make the sweet cream
foam and serve with the mousse.

Preparation time **35 minutes**
Cooking time **5 minutes**
Level **difficult**

pistachio semifreddo

Ingredients for 4 servings
Semifreddo:

1½ oz (40 g) extra-dark chocolate
2 cups (2 oz or 60 g) chocolate
puffed rice
7 oz (200 g) pistachio ice cream
1/2 cup (120 ml) whipping cream

Decoration:

4 blackcurrant or redcurrant sprigs
dark chocolate, shaved

Line a baking sheet with plastic wrap.
Place 4 individual spring-form molds (without the bottom)
on the baking sheet.
Melt the chocolate over a double boiler. Pour the melted
chocolate over the puffed rice and mix well.
Place 1 tablespoon of the rice mixture in each spring-from
mold. Use a spatula to make an even layer.
Place the ice cream in a bowl and mix it with a spatula
until creamy. Whip the whipping cream and incorporate
it into the ice cream. Fill the spring-from molds with
the ice cream mixture and refrigerate for 30 minutes.
Remove from the refrigerator and unmold the
semifreddos.
Place each semifreddo on a serving plate and decorate
with currant sprigs and chocolate shavings.

Desserts

126

For an aromatic touch, mix
1 tablespoon Maraschino liqueur
into the pistachio ice cream.

Preparation time **25 minutes**
Cooking time **3 minutes**
Level **medium**

chestnut, chocolate and celeriac cake

Ingredients for 4 servings

Chestnut and celeriac mousse:

1/2 cup (3 oz or 80 g) diced celeriac (celery root)

1½ cups (350 ml) milk, **1** vanilla bean

2 tbsps (1 oz or 30 g) butter

1/4 cup (60 ml) Amaretto liqueur

3½ oz (100 g) chestnut puree

2 egg yolks, **2** gelatin sheets

1/2 cup (3½ oz 100 g) sugar

1½ cups (300 ml) whipping cream, salt

Chocolate glaze:

3 tbsps whipping cream, **7** tbsps water

1/3 cup plus 1 tbsp (3 oz or 80 g) sugar

3½ oz (100 g) dark chocolate, chopped

3/4 cup (2 oz or 60 g) cocoa powder

Cake:

1 sponge cake (see p. 386)

1/4 cup (60 ml) dry sherry

10½ oz (300 g) chocolate cream

Boil the celeriac in the milk with the butter, vanilla bean and Amaretto liqueur for about 10 minutes.
Add the chestnut puree and pass the mixture through a sieve or food mill.
Beat the egg yolks with the sugar and a pinch of salt.
Soak the gelatin in cold water for a few minutes, drain and squeeze out the excess liquid. Add the gelatin and the egg yolk mixture to the chestnut-celeriac mixture.
Beat the whipping cream to stiff peaks and fold it into the mixture. Cover with plastic wrap and refrigerate.
Make the chocolate glaze: Boil the whipping cream with the sugar and water. Add the chocolate and cocoa powder and stir until smooth.
Place the sponge cake in a round cake pan and brush with the sherry. Cover with a thin layer of chocolate cream and a thick layer of the chestnut-celeriac mousse.
Refrigerate until firm, unmold and cover the entire cake with the chocolate glaze.

Preparation time **1 hour 30 minutes**
Cooking time **40 minutes**
Level **difficult**

Desserts

128

miniature chocolate cakes
with fruit skewers

Ingredients for 10 servings
Cakes:

6 eggs, separated

1¼ cups (250 g) sugar

1 cup (9 oz or 250 g) butter

9 oz (250 g) dark chocolate couverture

1 cup plus 3 tbsps (5½ oz or 150 g)
all-purpose flour

1/3 cup (2 oz or 50 g) cornstarch

Filling:

3½ oz (100 g) dark chocolate

2 tbsps (30 ml) whipping cream

2 tbsps (30 ml) glucose syrup

1/4 cup (20 g) cocoa powder

Sauces:

1 cup (250 ml) orange juice

9 oz (250 g) strawberries, **2** tbsps honey

Fruit:

seasonal fresh fruit

Beat the eggs with the sugar. Melt the butter and dark chocolate couverture and carefully stir it into the egg mixture. Sift in the flour and cornstarch and stir to combine. Pour the batter into 10 ramequins, filling them only half-full.
Melt the dark chocolate with the whipping cream.
Add the glucose syrup and cocoa powder.
Transfer the chocolate mixture to a pastry bag.
Pipe the chocolate mixture into the center of the chocolate cakes. Top with the remaining batter and freeze for 3-4 minutes to chill. Bake for 18-20 minutes.
Meanwhile cook the orange juice down until reduced to 1/2 cup (60 ml).
Puree the strawberries with the honey and strain them.
Thread the fresh fruit onto skewers, alternating contrasting colored fruit.
Unmold the hot cakes and place them on serving plates.
Decorate the plates with the orange and strawberry sauces. Add one fruit skewer to each plate and serve.

Preparation time **40 minutes**
Cooking time **20 minutes**
Level **difficult**

chocolate mousse with marrons glacé

Ingredients for 4 servings

Mousse:

1 gelatin sheet

2 tbsps water, **1** egg, separated

1/4 cup (1½ oz or 45 g) sugar

1/2 cup (125 ml) boiling milk

3½ oz (100 g) semi-sweet chocolate, chopped

1 tsp vanilla extract

2/3 cup (150 ml) whipping cream

salt

sponge cake strips (see p. 386) or ladyfingers

Decoration:

marrons glacé

(see p. 386)

If using home made sponge cake, try adding chopped almonds or almond flour to the batter for a delicious and rich variation.

Soak the gelatin sheet in cold water. Remove the gelatin and squeeze out the excess water.
Place in a small saucepan with the 2 tablespoons water and dissolve the gelatin over low heat.
Meanwhile, in a saucepan, beat the egg yolk and sugar until they become pale yellow and thick. Bring the milk to a boil and whisk into the egg mixture.
Return to the saucepan and cook over low heat until the cream thickens.
Remove from heat and stir in the gelatin, chocolate and vanilla. Let cool. Whip the cream and fold into the cooled chocolate mixture.Beat the egg white and a pinch of salt to form stiff peaks. Fold into the mousse.
Line the bottom of a serving bowl or trifle bowl with the sponge cake strips or ladyfingers. Pour the chocolate mousse over the cake and refrigerate for at least 2 hours. Garnish with marrons glace.

Preparation time **20 minutes**
Cooking time **10 minutes**
Level **easy**

Desserts

132

neapolitan-style trifle

Ingredients for 6 servings

Ingredients for 6 servings

Trifle:

1⅓ lb (600 g) sponge cake (see p. 386)

1/4 cup (60 ml) rum

10½ oz (300 g) ricotta

3/4 cup (5½ oz or 150 g) sugar

2 oz (60 g) extra-dark chocolate, finely chopped

1 tsp vanilla extract

Decoration:

3 egg whites

2½ tbsps confectioner's sugar

colored sprinkles

Cut the sponge cake horizontally into layers.
Brush each layer with the rum. The cake should be moist and very soft.
Stir the ricotta, sugar, chocolate and vanilla together.
Mix well to form a smooth cream.
Place a little sponge cake at the bottom of 6 small glass bowls. Top with a layer of the ricotta cream. Continue making alternating layers until all of the ingredients have been used up.
Beat the egg whites until they form stiff peaks.
Carefully fold in the confectioner's sugar.
Spread a layer of the meringue over the trifles, top with the colored sprinkles and refrigerate overnight.
Ladyfingers may be used in place of the sponge cake.

Preparation time **40 minutes**
Level **easy**

Desserts

italian chocolate trifle

Ingredients for 4 servings

Trifle:

2 egg yolks

2/3 cup plus 2 tbsps (5 oz or 140 g) sugar

1 tsp vanilla

1/4 cup (1 oz or 30 g) all-purpose flour

1 cup (250 ml) milk

3/4 cup plus 1 tbsp (200 ml) hot water

4 tbsps Alchermes liqueur

10½ oz (300 g) sponge cake (see p. 386)

2½ oz (70 g) dark chocolate, chopped

Beat the egg yolks and 1/3 cup (2 oz or 60 g) sugar together until thick and creamy. Add the vanilla and flour. Heat the milk in a saucepan. Whisk the hot milk into the egg mixture. Return to the saucepan and cook over low heat for at least 5 minutes.
Dissolve the remaining sugar in the hot water, add the Alchermes and let cool.
Brush the sponge cake rounds with the Alchermes syrup. Melt the chocolate over a double boiler. Make layers of the sponge cake, pastry cream and chocolate in a trifle bowl. Refrigerate for 2 hours before serving.

Trifle in Italian is known as zuppa inglese, "English soup," though some believe that its origins lie in the Italian Renaissance.

Preparation time **35 minutes**
Cooking time **10 minutes**
Level **easy**

individual yogurt mousses
with pear sauce

Ingredients for 4 servings
Pear sauce:
2 ripe Kaiser pears
juice from 1/2 lemon
1 tsp ground cinnamon
3 tbsps (1½ oz or 40 g) butter
3 Chinese peppercorns
1 tbsp apple juice concentrate
Yogurt mousse:
3/4 cup (7 oz or 200 g) plain yogurt
1 tbsp honey
1 gelatin sheet
1/3 cup (80 ml) whipping cream
1 egg white
salt
Decoration:
2 oz (50 g) dark chocolate

Core and dice the pears, leaving the skin on. Transfer the pears to a mixing bowl, pour over the lemon juice and sprinkle with cinnamon. Set aside.
Melt the butter in a small saucepan with the peppercorns and add the marinated pears. Cook for 5 minutes over medium-low heat and add the apple juice concentrate. Continue cooking until the pears are very tender.
Meanwhile, mix the yogurt with the honey. Soak the gelatin sheet in a little whipping cream and add it to the yogurt. Beat the egg white and a pinch of salt to stiff peaks. Beat the remaining whipping cream to stiff peaks. Fold the egg whites and whipped cream into the yogurt mixture. Divide the mixture between 4 cylindrical molds lined with parchment paper. Refrigerate until firm.
Melt the chocolate and spread it into a thin layer on a piece of waxed paper. Puree the pears in a food processor and pour the puree into 4 small bowls. Unmold the yogurt mousses and place one in each bowl.
Using a hot knife, cut the chocolate into squares and place one chocolate square on top of each mousse. Serve immediately.

Preparation time **50 minutes**
Cooking time **35 minutes**
Level **medium**

mont blanc

Ingredients for 6 servings
Mont Blanc:

3 lb (1½ kg) chestnuts

1 cup (250 ml) milk

2 cups (1 lb or 400 g) sugar

1/2 cup plus 1 tbsp (2 oz or 50 g) cocoa powder

2 tbsps rum

2 cups (500 ml) whipping cream

semi-sweet chocolate, shaved

Boil the chestnuts for about 45 minutes. Drain and peel. Using a food mill, puree the chestnuts and set aside. Heat the milk in a saucepan and stir in the sugar, cocoa powder and rum.
Pour the mixture over the chestnuts and stir to combine. Push the mixture through a potato ricer, letting the vermicelli-like strings fall directly onto a serving plate to form a mountain.
Whip the cream and use it to cover the chestnut strings. Alternatively transfer the whipped cream to a pastry bag and form small puffs around the outside of the chestnut puree. Sprinkle with shaved chocolate and serve cold.

Marrons glacé, whole or in small pieces, may be used to decorate the Mont Blanc along with candied violets and cherries. The dessert should be served chilled, but not too cold.

Preparation time **25 minutes**
Cooking time **45 minutes**
Level **easy**

chantilly cream cups
with chocolate cookies

Ingredients for 4 servings

Chantilly Cream:

4 egg yolks

2/3 cup (4½ oz or 125 g) sugar

1 tsp vanilla extract

1/3 cup plus 2 tbsps (2 oz or 50 g)
all-purpose flour

2 cups (500 ml) milk

3 tbsps whipping cream

5½ oz (150 g) semi-sweet chocolate

15-20 langues-de-chat cookies
(or other thin cookies)

1 tbsp pine nuts, toasted

Beat the egg yolks with a whisk until foamy
and then add the sugar and vanilla and mix well.
Add the flour and mix well.
Bring milk to a boil in a saucepan. Whisk the boiling
hot milk into the egg mixture. Return the mixture to the
saucepan and cook over low heat for 5 minutes to thicken.
Remove from the heat, pour into a bowl and refrigerate.
Whip the cream and refrigerate.
Melt the chocolate over a double boiler and dip
the langues-de-chat in the chocolate. Let them cool
on a tray lined with parchment paper. Reserve some
melted chocolate for decorating.
When the pastry cream is cool, fold in the whipped cream
with a wooden spoon.
Layer the chantilly cream and the remaining melted
chocolate in dessert cups or small bowls.
Top with toasted pine nuts and serve with chocolate-
coated cookies.

In cooking and baking, the term
thicken means to increase the density
of a sauce, soup or other liquid by
cooking off liquid or by adding a
thickener such as cornstarch, butter,
cream or egg yolks.

Preparation time **25 minutes**
Cooking time **15 minutes**
Level **medium**

chocolate bônet

Ingredients for 10 servings

Bônet:

4 cups (1 l) milk

3½ oz (100 g) ladyfingers

4 oz (120 g) small amaretto cookies

1/4 cup (60 ml) strong coffee

1 tbsp instant coffee

2 tbsps rum

2 tbsps Marsala wine, **5** eggs

1 cup (7 oz or 200 g) sugar

1/2 cup (2 oz or 50 g) cocoa powder

Bônet, also known as bunet, is a typical dessert from the Langhe region of Piedmont. The name means "beret" or "cap" in the local dialect. This may be because of the round molds sometimes used to make bônet. If desired, replace the amaretto cookies with crumbled torrone (nougat) or almond cookies.

Preheat the oven to 400°F (200°C or Gas Mark 6).
Bring the milk to a boil in a saucepan and let it cool.
Meanwhile, finely chop the ladyfingers with the amaretto cookies in a food processor or with a knife.
Add them to the milk. Stir in the coffee, instant coffee, rum and Marsala wine. Beat the eggs with the sugar and cocoa powder to obtain a smooth, thick cream.
Whisk the milk mixture into the egg mixture.
Sprinkle a pudding mold with sugar and heat on the stove for a few minutes, until the sugar begins to caramelize.
Remove from the heat and roll the mold around to evenly distribute the caramel. Set aside and let the caramel harden. Pour the batter into the mold and bake in a hot water bath in the oven for 40 minutes.
Remove from the heat and cool.
Serve cold or at room temperature.

Preparation time **15 minutes**
Cooking time **50 minutes**
Level **medium**

chocolate heart cake

Ingredients for 6 servings
Chocolate Heart:

3 oz (80 g) dark chocolate

11 tbsps (5½ oz or 150 g) butter

4 medium-sized butter cookies

1½ cups (7 oz or 200 g) almonds

2 eggs, separated

2/3 cup (4 oz or 120 g) sugar, salt

1 tbsp Strega liqueur

3/4 cup plus 1 tbsp (200 ml)
whipping cream

2 tbsps confectioners' sugar

1/2 tsp vanilla extract

cocoa powder

The almonds may be substituted
with 5½ oz (150 g) toasted hazelnuts,
increasing the amount of chocolate
by 3½ oz (100 g) and the sugar
by 3 tablespoons.

Preheat the oven to 350°F (180°C or Gas Mark 4).
Melt the chocolate over a double boiler with 3 tablespoons
butter and 2 tablespoons water, stirring frequently.
Blend the cookies and almonds together in a food
processor.
Beat the egg yolks with the sugar until thick and light
in color. Work the remaining butter with a spatula until
creamy and add it to the egg yolk mixture. Whisk in the
chocolate mixture, almond mixture and liqueur.
Whip the egg whites with a pinch of salt to stiff peaks
and fold into the batter.
Butter and flour a heart-shaped cake pan and pour in
the batter. Bake for 1 hour. Invert onto a wire rack to cool.
Whip the remaining whipping cream with the
confectioners' sugar and vanilla extract.
Slice the cake into 2 layers and spread 1 layer with
the whipped cream. Top with the second layer and sift
the cocoa powder over the top. Refrigerate until serving.

Preparazione **30 minuti**
Cottura **60 minuti**
Esecuzione **media**

chestnut cream roll
with chocolate glaze

Ingredients for 6 servings

Chestnut cream:

3 cups (700 ml) milk

1/4 cup (2 oz or 50 g) sugar

1 lb (400 g) peeled chestnuts

3/4 cup plus 1 tbsp (200 ml) whipping cream

1½ oz (40 g) dark chocolate

Cake:

1 sponge cake sheet, about 16 by 20
inches (40 by 50 cm) (see p. 386)

Glaze:

3½ oz (100 g) dark chocolate,
grated or shaved

1/2 cup (120 ml) whipping cream

Decoration:

white chocolate, shaved (optional)

⌐ If the purchased sponge cake is too
dry to roll, make a simple sugar
syrup, adding a little rum, and use
it to moisten the cake.

Place the milk, sugar and chestnuts in a large saucepan
and cook, covered, over low heat for 25 minutes, until
tender and creamy. Puree the mixture and let cool.
Beat the whipping cream to stiff peaks, fold it into
the chestnut cream and refrigerate. Meanwhile, place
the sponge cake on a large piece of parchment paper.
Spread the chestnut cream over the cake and grate
the dark chocolate over the cake.
Roll up the sponge cake like a jelly roll, using
the parchment paper to help tighten the roll.
Wrap in the parchment paper and refrigerate.
Meanwhile, make the glaze: Place the chocolate over
a double boiler and add the cream.
Heat until melted and let cool slightly. While the chocolate
glaze is cooled still fluid unwrap the chestnut roll
and pour the glaze over it, smoothing with a spatula
to make an even layer and coating the edges completely.
Refrigerate until the glaze hardens.
Serve, if desired, with white chocolate shavings.

Preparation time **30 minutes**
Cooking time **30 minutes**
Level **easy**

chestnut shakes

Ingredients for 4 servings

Chestnut:

1 cup (4½ oz or 130 g) chestnuts

1 tsp sugar

2/3 cup (150 ml) milk

1¼ cups (300 ml) whipping cream

2 tbsps confectioners' sugar

vanilla extract

ice cubes

semi-sweet chocolate, shaved

Make an X-shaped incision on each of the chestnuts and boil them in lightly sugared water. Drain and let cool. Peel the chestnuts.
Place chestnuts, milk, cream, confectioners' sugar and vanilla in a blender. Add a few cubes of ice and blend. Serve the chestnut shake in martini glasses with chocolate shavings.

Canned or vacuum-packed boiled chestnuts may be used in place of fresh chestnuts. Rinse the chestnuts well before proceeding with the recipe.

Preparation time **15 minutes**
Cooking time **20 minutes**
Level **easy**

dark chocolate tiny treats

Chocolate

muesli cookies
with chocolate glaze and ginger

Ingredients for 4 servings

Cookies:

1/2 cup (2½ oz or 70 g)
all-purpose flour

1½ cups (4½ oz or 130 g) muesli

3 tbsps rice malt

3 tbsps sesame oil, milk

Glaze:

2½ oz (70 g) dark chocolate

Decoration:

2 tbsps water, **1** tbsp rice malt

fresh ginger, sliced

Preheat the oven to 350°F (180°C or Gas Mark 4).
Mix together the flour and muesli. Add the rice malt,
oil and enough milk to form a compact dough.
Cover with plastic wrap and let rest for 20 minutes.
Roll out the dough on a lightly floured work surface
and cut out small cookies with a round cookie cutter.
Bake the cookies on an ungreased baking sheet
for 15 minutes. Remove from the oven and cool on wire
racks.Meanwhile heat the water and rice malt in a small
saucepan over high heat.
When the liquid becomes syrupy add the sliced ginger.
Stir to coat and remove the slices one by one.
Place the ginger on a baking sheet and let dry in a 180°F
(80°C or Gas Mark 1/4) oven for 1 hour 30 minutes.
Meanwhile, melt the chocolate over a double boiler.
Dip half of each cookie in the melted chocolate.
Place a few pieces of ginger on top of each one and let
the chocolate harden before serving.

Ginger is a wonderful spice to use
in the kitchen. It pairs well with
both sweet and savory foods. For a
delicious thirst-quenching drink,
mix pineapple, carrot and apple
juices and add a few teaspoons of
freshly grated ginger.

Preparation time **15 minutes**
Cooking time **1 hour 30 minutes**
Level **easy**

miniature spicy chocolate tarts

Ingredients for 4 servings

Crust:

10 tbsps (5½ oz or 150 g) butter, softened

1/2 cup (3½ oz 100 g) sugar

2 egg yolks

2⅓ cups plus 1 tbsp (10½ oz or 300 g) all-purpose flour

salt

Filling:

1 egg, **2/3** cup (4 oz or 120 g) sugar

7 oz (200 g) chile-flavored dark chocolate, chopped

2 gelatin sheets

7 tbsps whipping cream

Preheat the oven to 350°F (180°C or Gas Mark 4).
Cream the softened butter with the sugar. Add the egg yolks, flour and a pinch of salt. Mix together quickly and form into a ball. Cover with plastic wrap and refrigerate for 10 minutes. Roll out the dough until 3/4 inch (2 cm) thick.
Using a round cookie cutter, cut out 12½-inch (5 cm) rounds. Use the dough rounds to line 12 miniature tart tins and pierce the base with a fork. Bake for 10 minutes, remove from the oven, unmold and let cool.
Meanwhile, make the filling: Beat the egg and the sugar with an electric beater until thick and creamy.
Melt the chocolate over a double boiler.
Soak the gelatin in cold water for a few minutes.
Drain and squeeze out the excess water. Add the gelatin to the hot chocolate and stir with a wooden spoon.
Whisk the chocolate into the egg mixture until smooth.
Whip the whipping cream to stiff peaks and fold it into chocolate mixture.
Transfer the mousse to a pastry bag and pipe into the tart shells. Serve immediately.

Preparation time **30 minutes**
Cooking time **15 minutes**
Level **medium**

Chile-flavored chocolate can be found in specialty stores, or just add 1/2 teaspoon ground chili pepper to melted dark chocolate.

chocolate-vanilla caramels

Ingredients for 6 servings
Caramels:

5½ oz (150 g) vanilla-flavored dark chocolate, chopped

1 cup (250 ml) whipping cream

1¼ cups (9 oz or 250 g) sugar

2 tsps honey

1 tbsp (15 g) butter

Melt the chocolate over a double boiler. Heat the whipping cream in a small saucepan.

Caramelize 3 tablespoons sugar a small heavy-bottomed copper saucepan over low heat. Once the sugar has dissolved, add another tablespoon of sugar, and repeat until the sugar is gone. Slowly add the hot cream to the caramel and then the honey. Remove from the heat and pour in half of the chocolate. Return to heat and cook until it reaches 235°F (113°C). To see if the caramels are done without a candy thermometer, after 6-7 minutes of cooking, drop a small spoonful of caramel onto a plate and when it cools, test to see that it is the correct consistency.

Remove from heat and stir in the butter and remaining chocolate. Mix well and pour the caramel into a baking dish, smoothing it out into an even layer.

When cool, cut the caramel into small cubes and wrap them in greaseproof or wax paper.

Store in a sealed container.

If vanilla-flavored chocolate is unavailable, infuse the cream with 1 vanilla bean for 5 minutes before adding it to the caramel.

Preparation time **20 minutes**
Cooking time **40 minutes**
Level **difficult**

hazelnut-chocolate sandwich cookies

Ingredients for 8 servings

Cookies:

1⅔ cups (7 oz or 200 g)
all-purpose flour

14 tbsps (7 oz or 200 g)
margarine, softened

1 cup (7 oz or 200 g) sugar

2⅔ cups (7 oz or 200 g)
ground hazelnuts

Filling:

14 tbsps (7 oz or 200 g) margarine

1/4 cup (0.8 oz or 25 g) cocoa powder

1/2 cup (3½ or 100 g) raw cane sugar

1 tbsp rum

Preheat the oven to 375°F (190°C or Gas Mark 5).
Mix the flour and the softened margarine together.
Add the sugar and the ground hazelnuts. Mix well.
Line a baking sheet with parchment paper.
Roll the dough into small balls and place them
on the baking sheet. Bake for 20 minutes.
Meanwhile, mix the margarine, cocoa, sugar and rum
together to form a cream.
Let the hazelnut cookies cool completely and then spread
1 cookie with chocolate cream and stick it to another
cookie to form a sandwich.
Repeat with the other cookies.

The cocoa powder in the filling may
be substituted with chocolate cream
or hazelnut cream. The cookies may
be finished by rolling them in slivered
almonds or ground hazelnuts.

Preparation time **30 minutes**
Cooking time **20 minutes**
Level **easy**

Tiny Treats

chocolate-covered cherries

Ingredients for 4 servings

Cherries:

1¼ cups (9 oz or 250 g) sugar

3 tbsps cherry liqueur (kirsch)

1 tbsp glucose syrup

7 oz (200 g) dark couverture chocolate, chopped

16 small cherries preserved in alcohol

Mix the sugar, kirsch and glucose in a saucepan. Cook over medium heat until the syrup reaches 240°F (115°C). Pour the hot syrup onto a damp marble slab and let thicken. Spread with a spatula to form a thick paste. Keep working the paste with the spatula for a few minutes. Cut the paste into small pieces and place them in an airtight jar. Let sit for 1 day.
Reheat the kirsch mixture over a double boiler. Drain the cherries and add them to the kirsch mixture, stirring to coat evenly. Remove from the liquid and refrigerate for 30 minutes. Melt two-thirds of the chocolate over a double boiler, stirring frequently. Remove from heat and add the remaining chocolate. Stir until smooth. Dip the cherries in the melted chocolate one by one and let cool on a baking sheet lined with parchment paper.

Cherries and chocolate are a classic combination. Kirsch is a clear brandy distilled from cherry juice, named for the German word for cherry, Kirsche, which is believed to have originated in the Black Forest.

Preparation time **25 minutes**
Cooking time **10 minutes**
Level **difficult**

chocolate cream cookies

Ingredients for 6 servings

Cookies:

2 cups (9 oz or 250 g) all-purpose flour

2 eggs plus 1 egg yolk

2/3 cup (4½ oz 120 g) sugar

9 tbsps (4½ oz or 130 g) butter, diced

1 tsp vanilla extract

grated zest of 1 organic orange

Chocolate cream:

7 oz (200 g) dark chocolate

2/3 cup (150 ml) whipping cream

Decoration:

confectioners' sugar

For a crunchy variation, use only half the flour and add 1 cup (3½ oz or 100 g) chopped almonds. Make the filling by melting 7 oz (200 g) dark chocolate with 1/3 cup (3½ oz or 90 g) butter. Add 7 tbsps coffee. Whip 2/3 cup (150 ml) whipping cream and fold into the mixture.

Place the flour, eggs, egg yolk, sugar and butter in a large bowl. Add the vanilla extract and orange zest and work with the fingertips to obtain a smooth dough.
Form into a ball, cover with plastic wrap and refrigerate for 30 minutes.
Preheat the oven to 350°F (180°C or Gas Mark 4).
Roll out the dough into a very thin sheet on a lightly floured work surface. Using a round cookie cutter cut out as many rounds as possible. Place the rounds on a baking sheet and bake for 20 minutes.
Melt the chocolate over a double boiler, then let cool to room temperature.
Beat the whipping cream to stiff peaks, and fold it into the melted chocolate until thoroughly combined.
Pipe the chocolate cream onto half the cookies and the top with the remaining cookies to make sandwiches.
Dust with confectioners' sugar and serve.

Preparation time **25 minutes**
Cooking time **25 minutes**
Level **easy**

Tangy Treats

mint-chocolate covered strawberries

Ingredients for 6 servings

Strawberries:

5½ oz (150 g) mint-flavored dark chocolate, chopped

20 strawberries

Decoration:

mint leaves

Melt two-thirds of the chocolate over a double boiler or in the microwave at the lowest setting, taking care not to overcook it.
Remove from heat and add the remaining chocolate. Stir until melted.
Dip the strawberries in the melted chocolate.
Let any excess chocolate drip off, then place them on a baking sheet lined with parchment paper.
Sprinkle the strawberries with the chopped mint leaves and refrigerate until set. Serve cold.

For an elegant variation and a stunning visual effect, stick an edible gold leaf to each strawberry.

Preparation time **20 minutes**
Cooking time **10 minutes**
Level **easy**

rum-chocolate cups
with mascarpone cream

Ingredients for 4 servings
Chocolate cups:
1 egg white
3/4 cup (3 oz or 80 g) confectioners' sugar
1 tsp dark rum
1/3 cup (3 oz or 80 g) melted butter
1/3 plus 2 tbsps (3 oz or 80 g) all-purpose flour
4 tbsps cocoa powder
Cream:
4 oz (120 g) mascarpone
3½ oz (100 g) cream cheese
1 tbsp confectioners' sugar
1 tsp vanilla extract
Decoration:
1 basket of raspberries, mint leaves

The mascarpone may be substituted with 7 tbsps cream, lightly whipped.

Preheat the oven to 400°F (200°C or Gas Mark 6).
Beat the egg white and confectioners' sugar in a bowl and add the rum and melted butter.
Sift in the flour and cocoa powder and mix to form a sticky, elastic dough. Refrigerate for 20 minutes.
Line a baking dish with parchment paper.
Using the back of a spoon, spread the dough into circles 2½ inches (5 cm) in diameter. Bake for 5 minutes.
Remove from the oven and mold the chocolate rounds over upturned teacups or inside a muffin tin.
Let sit for 1 minute, then remove the chocolate cups and let them cool. Whip the mascarpone and cream cheese with the confectioners' sugar.
Transfer to a pastry bag and fill each chocolate cup.
Top with 1 raspberry and 1 mint leaf. Serve immediately.

Preparation time **30 minutes**
Cooking time **5 minutes**
Level **easy**

mini chocolate tarts
with marrons glacé

Ingredients for 8 servings

Mini Chocolate Tarts:

2½ oz (70 g) dark chocolate

2 oz (50 g) gianduia chocolate

1 egg plus 2 egg yolks

1 tbsp sugar, **1** tbsp rum

4 oz (120 g) marrons glacé, diced

3/4 cup plus 1 tbsp (200 ml)
whipping cream

10½ oz (300 g) shortcrust dough
(see note)

cocoa powder

To make the shortcrust dough place 2 1/3 cups (10½ oz or 300 g) flour, 1/2 cup (3½ oz or 100 g) sugar, 7 tbsps (5½ oz or 150 g) butter, 2 egg yolks, the grated zest of 1 lemon and a pinch of salt in a bowl. Mix together quickly with a fork and then using the fingertips to form a smooth dough. Roll into a ball and refrigerate for 30 minutes.

Melt the dark and gianduia chocolates together over a double boiler or in the microwave.
Beat the egg, egg yolks, sugar and rum over a double boiler until thick and foamy. Add the melted chocolate and the diced marrons glacé.
Beat the whipping cream to stiff peaks and fold it into the chocolate mixture. Freeze briefly to cool.
Cover with plastic wrap and refrigerate.
Preheat the oven to 350°F (180°C or Gas Mark 4).
Roll out the shortcrust dough on a lightly floured work surface and cut out several rounds with a cookie cutter.
Use the rounds to line miniature tart tins and bake until golden brown.
Remove from the oven and let cool.
Fill the cooled tart shells with the chocolate cream and dust with cocoa powder.
Serve chilled.

Preparation time **30 minutes**
Cooking time **30 minutes**
Level **medium**

peppered chocolate cherries

Ingredients for 4 servings
Cherries:

9 oz (250 g) pepper-flavored chocolate

1 tbsp sunflower oil

20 cherries, stems attached

1/3 cup (1 oz or 30 g) ground hazelnuts

Melt the chocolate with the sunflower oil over a double boiler, stirring frequently.

Place 20 paper baking cups or cylindrical silicon molds on a baking tray.

Pour a small spoonful of melted chocolate into each cup.

Place 1 cherry in the center of each cup, pushing down so that the chocolate nearly covers the cherry.

Sprinkle with ground hazelnuts and refrigerate until hard.

Remove the cherries from the cups before serving.

These cherries are ideal to serve at the end of a meal, accompanied by a cherry liqueur.

172

Pepper-flavored chocolate can be made by melting excellent quality dark chocolate with 1/2 teaspoon freshly ground black pepper.

Preparation time **10 minutes**
Cooking time **5 minutes**
Level **easy**

mini chocolate cakes
with strawberry centers

Ingredients for 4 servings

Cakes:

2 oz (50 g) extra-dark chocolate

1 tbsp whipping cream

3½ tbsps (2½ oz or 70 g) strawberry jam

3½ oz (100 g) dark chocolate

3 tbsps (3 oz or 80 g) butter

2 eggs

1/3 cup (2½ oz or 70 g) sugar

2 tbsps all-purpose flour

Preheat the oven to 400°F (200°C or Gas Mark 6). Melt the extra-dark chocolate with the cream over a double boiler. Add the strawberry jam and mix well. Transfer to the freezer and let harden slightly. Melt the remaining chocolate with the butter and let cool slightly. Beat the eggs and sugar until thick and creamy. Fold in the chocolate and butter mixture. Butter and flour 6 ramequins. Fill the ramequins two-thirds full with the chocolate batter. Remove the chocolate mixture from the freezer. Scoop out 6 balls using a melon baller and drop one ball into the center of each ramequin. Top with remaining batter. Bake for 12 minutes. Cool slightly and invert onto serving plates.

174

For a delicious winter dessert, substitute the strawberry jam with a chestnut or hazelnut cream or fill the center with white chocolate for a beautiful contrast.

Preparation time **15 minutes**
Cooking time **15 minutes**
Level **medium**

cocoa-rum cookies

Ingredients for 4 servings

Cookies:

1½ cups (3 oz or 90 g) blanched hazelnuts

1/2 cup (3½ oz or 100 g) sugar

3/4 cup plus 1 tbsp (3½ oz or 100 g) all-purpose flour

1/3 cup (1 oz or 30 g) cocoa powder

6 tbsps (3 oz or 80 g) butter, cut into small pieces

salt

1 tbsp dark rum

Preheat the oven to 350°F (180°C or Gas Mark 4).
Grind the hazelnuts with the sugar in a food processor.
Place the flour and cocoa powder in a mixing bowl.
Add the hazelnut mixture and butter.
Add a pinch of salt and pour over the rum.
Mix well to obtain a smooth dough.
Wrap in plastic wrap and refrigerate for 20 minutes.
Roll the dough into small walnut-sized balls, place on a baking sheet and press down lightly to flatten the bottom of the cookie.
Bake for 15 minutes, remove from the oven and cool completely on a wire rack.
Store in an air-tight container.

Rum dates back to the 16th century, around the time sugar cane was introduced to the Caribbean islands. Legend has that it was the preferred drink of the pirates who sailed the Caribbean seas, and that the name derives from the word rumbullion meaning "tumult" in the local dialect.

Preparation time **20 minutes**
Cooking time **15 minutes**
Level **easy**

baked chocolate-nut truffles

Ingredients for 6 servings

Truffles:

3/4 cup (3½ oz or 100 g) all-purpose flour

2/3 cup (7 oz or 200 g) honey

1¾ cups (5½ oz or 150 g) cocoa powder

2 oz (50 g) chocolate

1½ cups (10½ oz or 300 g) raisins

1⅓ cups (7 oz or 200 g) almonds

2 cups (7 oz or 200 g) chopped walnuts

1½ cups (7 oz or 200 g) hazelnuts

2/3 cup (3½ oz or 100 g) pine nuts

Preheat the oven to 400°F (200°C or Gas Mark 6).
Soak the raisins in warm water for 10 minutes.
Drain and squeeze out any excess water.
Soak the almonds and hazelnuts in warm water
for a few minutes and then dry them on a clean kitchen
towel, removing the skins.
Place all of the nuts and the raisins in a mortar and pestle
and grind them into a coarse meal.
Heat the honey over low heat until liquid.
Place the ground nut mixture in a large mixing bowl
and add the flour, cocoa powder, grated chocolate
and honey. Mix with a wooden spoon to combine,
forming a dense dough.
Roll the dough into little balls and place them on a baking
sheet. Bake for 30 minutes.

For a tasty variation, soak the raisins in Passito wine or a liqueur before using.

Preparation time **40 minutes**
Cooking time **30 minutes**
Level **easy**

sweet ravioli

Ingredients for 4 servings

Dough:

4¾ cups (1⅓ lb or 600 g) all-purpose flour

4 eggs, **1** tsp baking powder

3/4 cups (5½ oz or 150 g) sugar

9 tbsps (4½ oz or 125 g) butter, softened

grated zest of **1/2** orange

grated zest of **1/2** lemon

Filling:

12½ oz (350 g) ricotta

1/2 cup (3 oz or 90 g) sugar

3 oz (90 g) extra-dark chocolate, chopped

1 candied citron, chopped

2 tbsps pine nuts

1/2 tsp ground cinnamon

1/4 cup (60 ml) orange liqueur

Mound the flour on a work surface and make a well in the center. Add the eggs and sugar and mix. Add the butter, orange and lemon zest and baking powder and continue kneading until the dough is smooth. Let the dough rest. Meanwhile, sieve the ricotta. Mix the ricotta with the sugar in a bowl. Add the chocolate, citron, pine nuts, cinnamon and liqueur. Mix until smooth. Knead the dough for a few minutes. Lightly flour a work surface and roll the dough out into 2 thin rectangular sheets. Drop the filling in rounded teaspoonfuls along the center of a sheet, at least 2 inches (5 cm) apart. Cover with the second sheet of pasta and press down along the edges and between each round of filling. Cut into ravioli. Butter a baking sheet and place the ravioli on the sheet. Bake for 20 minutes and cool completely. If you desire, sprinkle with confectioners' sugar and serve with whipped cream.

Preparation time **1 hour 30 minutes**
Cooking time **20 minutes**
Level **medium**

mini citrus-yogurt cups

Ingredients for 4 servings

Cups:

10½ oz (300 g) shortcrust dough (see p. 386)

1 cup (9 oz or 250 g) plain low-fat yogurt

1 tbsp confectioners' sugar

1/2 tsp vanilla extract

grated zest of 1 organic orange

grated zest of 1 organic lemon

3½ oz (100 g) dark chocolate

2 ripe apricots, pitted and diced

Preheat the oven to 325°F (170°C or Gas Mark 3).
Roll out the shortcrust dough into a thin sheet and cut out rounds with a cookie cutter. Place the rounds in miniature tart tins or semi-spherical molds.
Pierce the dough with a fork and bake for 10 minutes.
Remove from the oven, unmold and cool completely.
Mix together the yogurt, sugar, vanilla and citrus zest.
Melt the chocolate over a double boiler.
Dip the outside of the pastry cups into the chocolate and set on a wire rack to harden.
Once cooled, fill the cups with the yogurt mixture and place one piece of apricot in each cup. Serve cold.

182

To prevent the formation of air pockets while baking the pastry cups, cover the unbaked dough with wax paper and fill with dried beans, uncooked rice or pie weights.

Preparation time **45 minutes**
Cooking time **10 minutes**
Level **easy**

mini chocolate-almond tarts

Ingredients for 6 servings

Pastry:

1/2 tsp active dry yeast

1 tbsp warm milk

4¾ cups (1⅓ lb or 600 g) all-purpose flour

7 tbsps (3½ oz or 100 g) butter

2/3 cup (4 oz or 120 g) sugar

2 eggs plus 4 egg yolks

grated zest of 1 lemon

Filling:

1 cup (5½ oz or 150 g) toasted almonds

10½ oz (300 g) dark chocolate, chopped

5 tbsps grape jam

1 tbsp bitter herb liqueur, like Centerbe

ground cinnamon

Centerbe liquor may be substituted with an anise liqueur like Pastis.

Preheat the oven to 400°F (200°C or Gas Mark 6).
Dissolve the yeast in the warm milk.
Sift the flour onto a work surface and make a well at the center. Add the butter, sugar, yeast mixture, eggs, egg yolks and lemon zest. Mix together to form a smooth and compact dough. Roll out the dough into a thin sheet and cut out rounds with a cookie cutter.
Place half of the rounds in miniature tart tins. Reserve the other half for the top of the tarts.
Make the filling: Grind the almonds in a food processor and transfer to a mixing bowl. Add the chopped chocolate, jam, liqueur and a pinch of cinnamon. Mix well to form a very thick mixture.
Place 1 teaspoon of filling in each tart and cover the tarts with the reserved dough rounds. Pinch the edges to seal and bake for 15 minutes.
Sprinkle with confectioners' sugar, if desired, and serve.

Preparation time **30 minutes**
Cooking time **20 minutes**
Level **easy**

mostaccioli cookies

Ingredients for 8 servings
Cookies:

⅔ cups (14 oz or 400 g) blanched almonds

2 oz (50 g) dark chocolate

8 cups (2 lb 3 oz or 1 kg) all-purpose flour

1¼ cups (3½ oz or 100 g) cocoa powder

1/2 cup (3½ oz or 100 g) lard or shortening, softened

2 tsps baking powder

2½ cups (1 lb or 500 g) sugar

4 cups (1 l) vin cotto (see note)

1 pat of butter

Glaze:

2 cups (500 ml) water

1 cup (7 oz or 200 g) sugar

Vin cotto is a syrupy liquid made from cooking down unfermented grape juice. It can be found in some specialty stores.

Preheat the oven to 350°F (180°C or Gas Mark 4). Toast the almonds in the oven for 10 minutes. Let cool and chop coarsely. Melt the chocolate over a double boiler or in the microwave. Place the flour in a large mixing bowl and add the almonds, cocoa powder, melted chocolate, softened lard, baking powder and sugar.

Mix to incorporate all of the ingredients and add enough vin cotto to make a compact dough.

Form the dough into small irregular balls and place on a buttered baking sheet. Bake for 20 minutes.

Mostaccioli cookies may be preserved for up to 2 weeks in an airtight container.

Before serving, glaze the cookies with a sugar syrup made by boiling 2 cups (500 ml) water with 1 cup (7 oz or 200 g) sugar.

Preparation time **25 minutes**
Cooking time **20 minutes**
Level **easy**

strawberry mousse
in chocolate cups

Ingredients for 8 servings
Mousse:

5½ oz (150 g) strawberries, hulled

1/3 cup (2 oz or 60 g) sugar

1 tbsp white rum

1 gelatin sheet

1 cup plus 3 tbsps (280 ml) whipping cream

7 oz (200 g) dark chocolate couverture

chocolate sauce

Place half of the strawberries and all of the sugar in a frying pan and sauté for a few minutes.
Add the rum and cook for a few minutes. Remove from the heat. Soak the gelatin in cold water.
Drain and squeeze out the excess water.
Add the gelatin to the cooked strawberries.
Add the uncooked strawberries and puree in a blender or food processor.
Whip the whipping cream to stiff peaks and fold into the strawberry mixture. Refrigerate.
Melt the chocolate over a double boiler or in a microwave.
Coat the inside of 20 waxed paper cups with melted chocolate. Refrigerate the cups until the chocolate hardens, then remove from the paper.
Fill the chocolate cups with strawberry mousse and drizzle with chocolate sauce. Chill before serving.

Frozen strawberries or raspberries may be used for the puree. If desired, decorate the mousse cups with fresh strawberries.

Preparation time **30 minutes**
Cooking time **10 minutes**
Level **medium**

panpepato

Ingredients for 6-8 servings

Panpepato:

2/3 cup (3½ oz or 100 g) raisins

1 cup (3½ oz or 100 g) walnuts

3/4 cup (3½ oz or 100 g) hazelnuts

2/3 cup (3½ oz or 100 g) blanched almonds

5½ oz (150 g) dark chocolate

3½ oz (100 g) candied fruit

nutmeg, grated, pepper

2 tsps ground cinnamon

2/3 cup (200 ml) honey

all-purpose flour

Preheat the oven to 350°F (180°C or Gas Mark 4).
Soak the raisins in warm water for a few minutes.
Drain and squeeze out the excess water.
Finely chop the walnuts, hazelnuts, almonds, chocolate
and candied fruit and mix together. Add a pinch of nutmeg,
pepper, the cinnamon and raisins.
Heat the honey and a little water in a saucepan and bring
to a boil. Pour the boiling honey over the nut mixture.
Mix until the chocolate melts and then sift in enough flour
to make the mixture come together to a dough.
Form the dough into 6 rounds and place them
on a parchment paper-lined baking sheet.
Bake for 10 minutes.
Remove from the oven and cool completely before serving.
The panpepato may be stored for up to 2 weeks
in an air-tight container.

Panpepato is a traditional Tuscan
dessert. Chocolate was added to the
recipe after it appeared in the Old World
following the discovery of the Americas.

Preparation time **10 minutes**
Cooking time **20 minutes**
Level **medium**

chocolate beignets

Ingredients for 6 servings
Filling:
9 oz (250 g) dark chocolate
1 cup (250 ml) whipping cream
Beignets:
1½ tbsps water
3½ tbsps milk
2 tbsps (1 oz or 25 g) butter
1/3 cup plus 1 tbsp (50 g) all-purpose flour
2 eggs
Decoration:
3½ oz (100 g) dark chocolate

For a stronger-flavored filling, add 1/4 cup (60 ml) espresso coffee or 2 tbsps rum or other liqueur to the melted chocolate.

Preheat the oven to 425°F (220°C or Gas Mark 7). Melt the chocolate for the filling over a double boiler. Whip the whipping cream into stiff peaks and fold it into the chocolate.
Meanwhile, bring the water and milk to a boil with the butter. Remove from the heat and add the flour little by little, stirring constantly with a wooden spoon. Return to heat and cook for 2 minutes, stirring continuously. Let cool and add the eggs one at a time. Using a spoon form 24 small balls of the mixture and place them on a buttered baking sheet.
Bake for 6-7 minutes, until the beignets have risen, then turn the heat down to 375°F (190°C or Gas Mark 5) to finish cooking.
Remove from the oven, let cool and slice in half horizontally. Transfer the chocolate cream to a pastry bag and fill the beignets with the cream. Melt the remaining chocolate and drizzle it over the beignets before serving.

Preparation time **50 minutes**
Cooking time **20 minutes**
Level **medium**

mini layered cream tarts

Ingredients for 4 servings

Crust:

2 cups (9 oz or 250 g) all-purpose flour

2 cups (2 oz or 50 g) multigrain cereal flakes

2/3 cup (4 oz or 120 g) sugar

1 egg

1/2 cup (4 oz or 120 g) butter

1 tsp vanilla extract

Filling:

1 cup (250 ml) milk

1/2 vanilla bean, sliced lengthwise

2 egg yolks

1/3 cup (2 oz or 60 g) sugar

1/4 cup (1 oz or 30 g) all-purpose flour

3½ oz (100 g) dark chocolate

To save time, use purchased shortcrust tart shells for this recipe.

Place all of the ingredients for the crust in a large bowl and mix together using the fingertips.
When the dough comes together, transfer it to a clean work surface and knead briefly with the palm of the hand.
Roll into a ball, wrap in plastic wrap and refrigerate.
Bring the milk and vanilla bean to a boil, then discard the vanilla bean.
Beat the egg yolks with the sugar until they are thick and pale yellow in color. Sift in the flour and mix.
Slowly drizzle the hot milk into the egg mixture, whisking constantly. Return to the stove and cook over medium heat until the cream coats the back of a spoon.
Divide the cream between two bowls and add the chocolate to one, stirring until melted.
Preheat the oven to 350°F (180°C or Gas Mark 4).
Roll out the crust dough and cut it into 4 rounds.
Use the dough to line 4 small tart tins. Pierce with a fork and bake for 12 minutes. Remove from the oven and cool.
Unmold the tarts and fill them half with the pastry cream, then finish with the chocolate cream.

Preparation time **40 minutes**
Cooking time **30 minutes**
Level **easy**

chocolate-covered torrone

Ingredients for 6 servings
Torrone:

3/4 cup (3½ oz 100 g) hazelnuts

2/3 cup (3½ oz or 100 g) blanched almonds

1 cup (7 oz or 200 g) sugar

7 tbsps water

1 egg

sunflower oil

7 oz (200 g) dark chocolate

Grind the hazelnuts and almonds in a food processor. Heat the sugar and water in a small saucepan and boil for 5 minutes or until it reaches 250°F (120°C). The syrup should be thick and soft.
Add the ground nuts and mix with a wooden spoon over low heat. Let cool slightly, add the egg and return to the heat. Cook for 2 more minutes.
Oil a baking sheet with the sunflower oil. Pour the torrone onto the baking sheet and spread into an even layer using a spatula. Let cool and cut into small squares.
Melt the chocolate over a double boiler. Dip the torrone in the chocolate and place on a wire rack to cool.

Keep the torrone in an air-tight container for a few days or store in the freezer for up to 2 weeks.

Preparation time **20 minutes**
Cooking time **15 minutes**
Level **medium**

chocolate-chestnut fritters

Ingredients for 4 servings
Dough:
4 cups (1 lb or 450 g) all-purpose flour

2 eggs, salt, **1** tbsp baking soda

6 tbsps (3 oz or 80 g) butter, softened

3/4 cup (5½ oz or 150 g) sugar, milk

2 cup (500 ml) extra-virgin olive oil

Filling:
9 oz (250 g) chestnuts, boiled and peeled

3½ oz (100 g) dark chocolate, chopped

1/3 cup (2 oz or 50 g) almonds, chopped

2 oz (50 g) candied fruit, diced

zest of **1** lemon

Decoration:
confectioners' sugar

Mix together the flour, eggs, a pinch of salt, softened butter and sugar. Add enough milk to form a smooth dough. Let the dough rest for 1 hour.
Dilute the baking soda in a little warm milk and add it to the dough. Puree the chestnuts and place in a bowl. Add the chopped chocolate, almonds, candied fruit and lemon zest. Mix to incorporate. The filling should be fairly dense. Roll out the dough into a very thin sheet. Using a round cookie cutter, cut out as many rounds as possible. Place a teaspoon ful of filling on each round and fold it into a half moon shape.
Pinch the edge to seal. Heat equal parts of olive oil in a saucepan and deep fry the fritters until golden brown. Drain on paper towels, sprinkle with confectioners' sugar and serve very hot.

The fritters may also be filled with plum or cherry jam.

Preparation time **40 minutes**
Cooking time **20 minutes**
Level **easy**

blueberry and chocolate pastries

Ingredients for 4 servings

Dough:

2 eggs

3 tbsps grappa

1/3 cup (2½ oz or 75 g) sugar

3 tbsps (2 oz or 50 g) melted butter, salt

2⅓ cups (10½ oz or 300 g) all-purpose flour

Filling:

1 basket of blueberries

2 oz (60 g) dark chocolate, chopped

2 cups (500 ml) sunflower oil

confectioners' sugar

Mix the eggs, grappa, sugar, melted butter and salt together. Whisk in the flour.

Mix to form a smooth and elastic dough. Cover the dough with plastic wrap and refrigerate for 30 minutes.

Roll out the dough into a thin sheet and cut out circles with a cookie cutter.

Place 2 blueberries on each round and sprinkle with chocolate.

Fold each in half and press down on the edges to seal.

Heat the sunflower oil in a saucepan and fry the pastries.

Drain on paper towels and sprinkle with confectioners' sugar.

Blueberries are a summer fruit, available from June to September. Their fresh taste makes them an ideal addition to many recipes. Blueberries may be preserved in delicious sauces and jams or frozen for later use.

Preparation time **25 minutes**
Cooking time **10 minutes**
Level **easy**

hazelnut tartlets
with chocolate ganache

Ingredients for 6 servings

Pastry:

1/2 cup (2½ oz or 75 g) hazelnuts

1/2 cup (3½ oz or 100 g) sugar

7 tbsps (3½ oz or 100 g) butter

2 egg yolks

1¼ cups (5½ oz or 150 g)
all-purpose flour

salt

Ganache:

7 oz (200 g) dark chocolate (80% cocoa)

1/3 cup (80 ml) whipping cream

Decoration:

ground hazelnuts

Grind the hazelnuts with the sugar in a food processor
until they are the consistency of flour.
Quickly mix together the butter, hazelnut mixture,
egg yolks, flour and pinch of salt with the fingertips.
Roll the dough into a ball and wrap in plastic wrap.
Refrigerate for 1 hour.
Preheat the oven to 350°F (180°C or Gas Mark 4).
Roll out the dough on a lightly floured work surface.
Butter and flour 6 small tartlet tins and line them with
the dough. Pierce the dough with a fork and cover each
tart with parchment paper. Fill the tarts with dried beans
or pie weights and bake for 15 minutes.
Cool on a wire rack.
Meanwhile, melt the chocolate over a double boiler
or in the microwave. Whisk in the cream.
Place a spoonful of ganache in the center of each tartlet
shell. Let cool and sprinkle with the ground hazelnuts.

Tangy Treats

202

Nuts should always be ground with
sugar as the sugar absorbs the oils
that could, when released,
create a bitter aftertaste.

Preparation time **25 minutes**
Cooking time **15 minutes**
Level **easy**

chocolate and vanilla phyllo parcels

Ingredients for 4 servings

Parcels:

4 egg yolks

2/3 cup (4 oz or 125 g) sugar

1 tsp vanilla extract

1/2 cup (2 oz or 60 g) all-purpose flour

2 cups (500 ml) milk

2 oz (50 g) extra dark chocolate, chopped

8 phyllo dough sheets

2 cups (500 ml) sunflower oil

Decoration:

mascarpone or vanilla ice cream

2 canned peaches in syrup, drained and sliced

Beat the egg yolks with the sugar and vanilla extract. Add the flour and mix well.

Bring the milk to a boil and whisk it into the egg mixture. Return the mixture to the heat and cook, stirring constantly, until the cream thickens and coats the back of a spoon. Divide the cream into 2 bowls and add the chopped chocolate to one.

Stir the cream until the chocolate dissolves.

Refrigerate until the creams cool and harden.

Spread out the sheets of phyllo on a work surface.

Place a spoonful of cream on each sheet of dough, using only one type of cream per sheet of dough.

Pull up the 4 corners and tie the parcel closed with a short length of kitchen string.

Heat the oil and fry the chocolate and vanilla parcels until golden-brown. Drain on paper towels.

Remove the string.

Serve the parcels with a scoop of ice cream and a slice of peach.

If phyllo dough is unavailable, won-ton wrappers or briq dough may be used instead.

Preparation time **40 minutes**
Cooking time **30 minutes**
Level **medium**

chocolate torrone

Ingredients for 6 servings

Torrone:

1 cup plus 2 tbsps (5½ oz or 150 g) hazelnuts

5 egg whites

salt

3/4 cup (5½ oz or 150 g) sugar

5 tbsps water

10½ oz (300 g) dark chocolate, chopped

1/2 cup (150 g) honey

edible wafer paper

Toast the hazelnuts in the oven for 10 minutes. Let cool, then use a clean kitchen towel to rub off the skins.
Beat the egg whites and a pinch of salt to stiff peaks.
In a small pan, heat half the sugar with all the water, stirring with a wooden spoon until dissolved.
Add the chocolate to the syrup and stir until melted.
In another saucepan, heat the honey until a drop congeals when dripped into a glass of cold water.
Caramelize the remaining sugar with a little water in another small pan. Remove from the heat and add the honey, egg whites, chocolate mixture and the hazelnuts. Mix to form an even batter.
Place 1 sheet of wafer paper on a work surface and pour on the torrone batter.
Spread into a layer 2/3 inch (2 cm) thick and top with another wafer sheet.
Cover and let cool. Once cool, but not completely hardened, cut the torrone into small rectangles.

Edible wafer paper is frequently used in candy making. It can be found at specialty stores.

Preparation time **45 minutes**
Cooking time **20 minutes**
Level **medium**

chocolate truffles

Ingredients for 4 servings
Truffles:
1/2 pandoro
3/4 cup plus 1 tbsp (200 ml) milk
1 tbsp Amaretto liqueur
1½ oz (50 g) amaretto cookies
3 oz (80 g) dark chocolate
3 tbsps whipping cream
Decoration:
1/2 cup (2 oz or 60 g)
unsalted pistachios
1/4 cup (1 oz or 20 g) sliced almonds

Dice the pandoro and soak it in the milk and Amaretto liqueur. Let sit for 5 minutes. Squeeze out the excess liquid and transfer the soaked pandoro to a bowl.
Crumble in the amaretto cookies and mix well.
Roll small quantities of the mixture into balls.
Cover and refrigerate until firm.
Melt the chocolate in a double boiler with the whipping cream. Mix well and let cool.
Finely chop the pistachios in a food processor and toast the almonds.
Form a piece of greaseproof paper into a cone in the palm of the hand. Fill with the chocolate mixture, then cut a small hole in the tip of the cone.
Drizzle the chocolate over the truffles and sprinkle with the pistachios and almonds.

Greaseproof, parchment and wax papers are used to preserve foods in the refrigerator or to line baking trays so that foods will not stick during baking.

Preparation time **20 minutes**
Cooking time **10 minutes**
Level **easy**

chocolate cookies
with cinnamon cream

Ingredients for 4 servings

Cookies:

2/3 cup (3 oz or 90 g) hazelnuts

1/2 cup (3½ oz or 100 g) sugar

4 tbsps (2 oz or 60 g) butter

2 tbsps dark rum, **2** egg yolks

3 tbsps whipping cream

5 tsps cocoa powder

1/3 cup (1½ oz or 45 g)
all-purpose flour

Cream:

2 cups (500 ml) whole milk

2 cinnamon sticks, **4** egg yolks

2/3 cup (4 oz or 120 g) sugar

2/3 cup (3 oz or 80 g) all-purpose flour

Decoration:

1 oz (30 g) dark chocolate

If desired, replace the cinnamon in the
cream with a grated pecan nut.

Preheat the oven to 425°F (220°C or Gas Mark 7).
Toast the hazelnuts in the oven. Grind two-thirds
of the nuts with the sugar in a food processor.
Mix together the butter, hazelnut mixture, rum, whipping
cream and cocoa powder. Lightly beat the egg whites
and add them to the mixture. Sift in the flour and stir
to incorporate. Chop the remaining hazelnuts.
Place spoonfuls of batter on a baking sheet lined
with greaseproof paper. Spread each spoonful into a thin
layer using the back of a spoon. Sprinkle the chopped
hazelnuts over the batter and bake for 4-5 minutes.
Mold the hot cookies over the back a rolling pin.
Bring the milk and the cinnamon sticks to a boil. Beat
the egg yolks with the sugar until thick and pale yellow.
Sift in the flour and mix to incorporate. Remove the
cinnamon sticks from the milk and whisk the hot milk into
the egg mixture. Return to the saucepan and cook over
medium heat until the cream coats the back of a spoon.
Remove from the heat and let cool in the refrigerator.
Melt the chocolate and drizzle it over the cooled cookies.
Serve the cookies with the cold cinnamon cream.

Preparation time **30 minutes**
Cooking time **15 minutes**
Level **medium**

chocolate chip muffins

Ingredients for 6 servings
Muffins:

9 tbsps (4½ oz or 125 g) butter

1/2 cup (3 oz or 90 g) sugar

2 tbsps raw cane sugar

2 eggs, **1** tsp vanilla extract

1⅔ cups (7 oz or 200 g)
all-purpose flour

1 tbsp cocoa powder

salt

2/3 cup (150 ml) milk

1 tsp baking powder

1/3 cup (2 oz or 60 g) dark chocolate
chips

Preheat the oven to 375°F (190°C or Gas Mark 5).
Cream the butter and gradually add both sugars.
Beat the eggs and vanilla together and add to the butter
and sugar.
Sift the flour, cocoa powder and salt together. Add a third
of the flour mixture, stir, and then add a third of the milk.
Continue adding the flour mixture and milk alternately
until both are finished. Add the baking powder and then
the chocolate chips. Stir to combine.
Pour the batter into paper muffin cups, filling them
two-thirds full.
Bake for 20 minutes. Let cool and serve.

If the paper muffin cups seem
too thin, use two together.
Alternatively, use aluminum
muffin cups.

Preparation time **15 minutes**
Cooking time **20 minutes**
Level **easy**

molten chocolate-cherry cake with almond granita

Ingredients for 4 servings

Granita:
2/3 cup (150 ml) almond milk
2/3 cup (150 ml) water

Cake:
2 oz (50 g) milk chocolate
1 tbsp whipping cream
1/3 cup (3½ oz or 100 g) cherry jam
2 eggs
1/3 cup (2½ oz or 70 g) sugar
1 tbsp all-purpose flour
6 tbsps (3 oz or 80 g) butter
3½ oz (100 g) dark chocolate

Decoration:
cherries, mint

Almond milk is prepared with sweet and bitter almonds, sugar and orange water. It can be made at home by diluting 1 part almond paste with 6 parts water.

Preheat the oven to 400°F (200°C or Gas Mark 6).
Mix the almond milk and water together and freeze in an ice cream maker.
Melt the milk chocolate with the cream and stir in the cherry jam. Pour the mixture into a baking dish and place in the freezer.
Beat the eggs with the sugar and sift in the flour. Melt the butter and dark chocolate together and add it to the egg mixture. Butter 8 miniature ramequins and, using a pastry bag, fill the ramequins half full with the chocolate batter.
Remove the chocolate-cherry mixture from the freezer and cut it into small squares. Place one square in each ramequin. Bake the cakes for 10 minutes.
Remove the cakes from the oven.
Unmold and decorate with the cherries and mint leaves.
Serve the cakes with the almond granita.

Preparation time **20 minutes**
Cooking time **10 minutes**
Level **medium**

chocolate truffles
with coconut and rum

Ingredients for 4 servings

Truffles:

3½ oz (100 g) extra dark chocolate, chopped

9 oz (250 g) ricotta

ground chili pepper

3 tbsps (1½ oz or 40 g) sugar

1 tsp vanilla extract

1 tbsp dark rum

1/2 cup (2 oz or 50 g) shredded coconut

Decoration:

shredded coconut

Melt the chocolate in a microwave, stirring frequently, or over a double boiler without letting the water boil. Sieve the ricotta and then beat it with a pinch of ground chili pepper and the sugar. Add the vanilla and rum and mix well. Slowly stir in the melted chocolate. Add the coconut and mix quickly to combine before the chocolate begins to harden.
Refrigerate for 30 minutes.
Form the chilled mixture into cherry-sized balls and place them on a baking sheet.
Roll the truffles in the remaining shredded coconut and refrigerate for 10 minutes before serving.

This recipe's Mexican origins are apparent in the pairing of chocolate and chili pepper, a popular combination among pre-Colombian civilizations. For another spicy variation, try substituting the chili pepper with the same amount of ground ginger.

Preparation time **20 minutes**
Cooking time **5 minutes**
Level **easy**

almond-coated chocolate truffles

Ingredients for 4 servings
Truffles:

7 oz (200 g) sponge cake (see p. 386)

3 tbsps rum

5½ oz (150 g) extra dark chocolate

1 cup (3 oz or 80 g) sliced almonds

Crumble the sponge cake into a mixing bowl and pour over the rum. Mix with fingertips and roll into little balls. Melt the chocolate over a double boiler, stirring frequently. Brush the sponge cake balls with the melted chocolate to form a thin layer.

Toast the sliced almonds in a non-stick pan over low heat until they color.

Roll the truffles in the almonds and set on a tray to cool. Serve the truffles after dinner with a dessert wine, if desired.

Panettone or any other leftover soft cake may be used in place of the sponge cake. The truffles may be enriched by adding candied orange peel or essential orange or almond oil.

Preparation time **15 minutes**
Cooking time **5 minutes**
Level **easy**

raspberry cream puffs
with chocolate sauce

Ingredients for 4 servings

Cream puffs:

1⅔ cups (7 oz or 200 g) raspberries

1/3 cup (2 oz or 60 g) sugar

3/4 cup plus 1 tbsp (200 ml) whipping cream

12 ready-made beignets

Chocolate sauce:

3½ oz (100 g) dark chocolate

6 tbsps whipping cream

1/3 cup (2 oz or 60 g) sugar crystals

Puree the raspberries with the sugar. Whip the whipping cream with a wire whisk and fold in the raspberry puree. Transfer the cream to a pastry bag and fill the beignets. Melt the chocolate with the cream in a double boiler. Remove from heat and let cool.
Coat the beignets with chocolate sauce and sprinkle with sugar crystals.
Refrigerate at least 1 hour before serving.

Preparation time **10 minutes**
Cooking time **3 minutes**
Level **easy**

dark chocolate log

Ingredients for 4 servings

Log:

7 tbsps (3½ oz or 100 g) melted butter

10½ oz (300) graham crackers, crushed

1/2 cup (3½ oz or 100 g) sugar

2 eggs

2/3 cup (2 oz or 60 g) cocoa powder

1/2 cup (60 ml) dry Marsala wine

1 handful pine nuts or almonds

Pour the melted butter over the crushed graham crackers. Add the remaining ingredients and mix well to combine. Pour the mixture onto a piece of aluminum foil and shape it into a log. Roll up the foil, forming the mixture into a log, and freeze for at least 2 hours.
Serve thickly sliced.

The graham crackers may be replaced with the same quantity of crushed meringues.

Preparation time **10 minutes**
Cooking time **2 minutes**
Level **easy**

mint-chocolate brownies

Ingredients for 6 servings

Brownies:

mint leaves

1 cup plus 1 tbsp (8 oz or 220 g) sugar

4½ oz (130 g) dark chocolate

8 tbsps (4 oz or 120 g) butter

1 cup plus 1 tbsp (8 oz or 220 g) raw cane sugar

2 eggs

2 tbsps mint liqueur

1¼ cups (6 oz or 160 g) all-purpose flour

1 cup (4½ oz or 125 g) almonds, chopped

Preheat the oven to 350°F (180°C or Gas Mark 4).
Chop a large handful of mint leaves and mix them with the sugar.
Melt the chocolate and butter over a double boiler.
Transfer to a mixing bowl and add the mint sugar and raw cane sugar. Lightly beat the eggs with the mint liqueur and add to the chocolate mixture.
Sift in the flour and add the chopped almonds. Mix well.
Pour the mixture into a parchment paper-lined baking dish and bake for 30 minutes.
Let cool and cut the brownies into squares.
Dust with confectioners' sugar if desired and serve.

224

The mint liquor may be replaced with orange liquor and the mint leaves with orange zest if desired.

Preparation time **30 minutes**
Cooking time **30 minutes**
Level **easy**

fried truffles with chocolate and ginger

Ingredients for 4 servings

Truffles:

6 tbsps whipping cream

2 tbsps (1 oz or 30 g) butter

1 piece of fresh ginger (about 1 inch or **2½** cm long), grated

7 oz (200 g) dark chocolate, chopped

2 tbsps chopped pistachios

2 tbsps chopped pine nuts

1/3 cup (2 oz or 50 g) almonds, chopped

1/3 cup (2 oz or 50 g) hazelnuts, chopped

2 tbsps cocoa nibs, sesame seeds

1 egg yolk, beaten, cocoa powder

ground chili pepper, sunflower oil

Bring the cream, butter and grated ginger to a boil in a saucepan. Remove from the heat, strain the mixture and add the chopped chocolate. Stir until the chocolate is melted. Transfer the mixture to a bowl and refrigerate until thickened.

Scoop out walnut-sized spoonfuls of the chocolate mixture and roll them into balls with the palms of the hands. Mix together the chopped nuts, coca nibs and sesame seeds. Roll the truffles in the nut mixture, then in the cocoa powder.

Dip in the beaten egg yolk and roll in the nut mixture one last time. Refrigerate for 1 hour.

Heat 2 cups (500 ml) sunflower oil in a saucepan, fry the truffles and drain on paper towels. Serve immediately.

Tiny Treats

226

The truffles may be served with a sauce made from 2 tablespoons honey, 7 tablespoons maple syrup, the juice of 1 lemon and a pinch of ground cinnamon. Heat briefly and let cool before serving.

Preparation time **30 minutes**
Cooking time **5 minutes**
Level **medium**

sponge cake sandwiches
with chocolate cream

Ingredients for 6 servings

Cake:

1 sponge cake round (see p. 386)

1 cup (250 ml) Alchermes liquor, sugar

Pastry cream:

4 egg yolks, **2** cups (500 ml) milk

2/3 cup (4½ oz or 125 g) sugar

1/3 plus **1** tbsp (2 oz or 50 g)
all-purpose flour

1 vanilla bean, halved lengthwise

Chocolate cream:

2 oz (50 g) dark chocolate, **4** egg yolks

3/4 cup (200 ml) whipping cream

2/3 cup (4½ oz or 125 g) sugar

Cut the sponge cake into small rounds and set aside.
Make the pastry cream: Beat the egg yolks with the sugar
until they are thick and pale yellow in color, sift in the flour
and stir to incorporate. Heat the milk and vanilla bean
in a saucepan. Strain the milk and whisk it into the egg
mixture. Return to the saucepan and cook over medium
heat until the cream coats the back of a spoon.
Remove from heat and set aside.
Make the chocolate cream: Melt the chocolate and cream
over a double boiler. Beat the egg yolks with the sugar
and add the melted chocolate. Beat until smooth.
Spread half of the sponge cake rounds with chocolate
cream and the other half with pastry cream.
Make sandwiches out of the sponge cake rounds.
Brush the exterior of the sandwiches with Alchermes
liquor and roll in sugar. Let sit until firm, then serve.

Sponge cake may be used in many
types of desserts, thanks to its soft
texture. In this recipe, the sponge cake
could be cut into any shapes desired.

Preparation time **30 minutes**
Cooking time **1 hour**
Level **medium**

milk and white chocolate cakes

chocolate

white chocolate cake with pears

Ingredients for 8 servings
Cake:

2 ripe pears

3/4 cup (6 oz or 165 g) raw cane sugar

3 tbsps grappa, 3 eggs, lightly beaten

2 cups (9 oz or 250 g) all-purpose flour

1 tsp baking powder

1/2 cup (4 oz or 120 g) melted butter

1/2 cup (120 ml) whipping cream, at room temperature

3½ oz (100 g) white chocolate

Caramel Glaze:

1/2 cup (3½ oz or 100 g) sugar

5 tbsps water

Preheat the oven to 350°F (180°C or Gas Mark 4).
Heat the sugar and water for the glaze in a small saucepan. Bring to a boil and cook to form a thin syrup.
Pour the glaze into the bottom of a high-rimmed round cake tin, spreading it evenly with a spoon.
Peel, core and slice the pears. Place them in a bowl and sprinkle over the raw cane sugar and the grappa.
Add the beaten eggs and sift over the flour and baking powder. Stir to incorporate all of the ingredients.
Add the melted butter and whipping cream.
Melt the chocolate in a double boiler. Add the chocolate to the cake batter and mix well.
Pour the batter into the prepared cake pan and bake for about 1 hour. Let cool completely and serve.

If there is any caramel glaze leftover, use it to decorate the serving plates for the cake.

Preparation time **40 minutes**
Cooking time **1 hour 5 minutes**
Level **medium**

walnut cake with chocolate glaze

Ingredients for 6 servings

Cake:

13 tbsps (6½ oz 185 g) butter

1/2 cup (3½ oz or 95 g) raw cane sugar

2 eggs, lightly beaten

1½ cups (6½ oz or 185 g) all-purpose flour

1 tsp baking powder, salt

6 tbsps milk

1 cup (3½ oz or 100 g) walnut halves

Chocolate glaze:

4 oz (120 g) milk chocolate

1 pat of butter

Preheat the oven to 350°F (180°C or Gas Mark 4).
Cream the butter and sugar in a mixer. Add the beaten eggs gradually.
Sift in the flour and baking powder and add a pinch of salt. Slowly pour in the milk and continue mixing until it has been completely incorporated.
Chop the walnuts and add 2/3 cup (2 oz or 60 g) to the batter. Butter and flour a round cake tin and pour in the batter. Bake for about 35 minutes.
Meanwhile, melt the chocolate and butter in a double boiler or in the microwave and then let cool until tepid, stirring constantly. Remove the cake from the oven and let cool slightly. Unmold the cake onto a wire rack and let cool completely. Pour the chocolate glaze over the cake and using a spatula, smooth the glaze evenly over the cake. Sprinkle over the remaining chopped walnuts.

Cakes

A richer version of this cake may be made by cutting the cake in half horizontally and filling it with chocolate ganache, made by adding whipping cream to the chocolate glaze.

Preparation time **30 minutes**
Cooking time **40 minutes**
Level **medium**

cinnamon cake with milk chocolate glaze

Ingredients for 8 servings

Cake:

2 cups (9 oz or 250 g) all-purpose flour

1 tsp baking powder

1 tbsp ground cinnamon

1¼ cups (9 oz or 250 g) sugar

2 eggs, **1** cup (250 ml) milk, salt

9 tbsps (4½ oz or 125 g) melted butter

Glaze:

3½ oz (100 g) milk chocolate

2 tbsps (30 ml) whipping cream

Decoration:

ground cinnamon (optional)

 For a variation with a surprise in the middle, pour two-thirds of the batter into the cake pan, sprinkle over 3 tablespoons raw cane sugar and 1/2 tablespoon ground cinnamon, then add the remaining batter. The sugar and cinnamon will caramelize while baking, making a sweet crust between the layers of cake.

Preheat the oven to 350°F (180°C or Gas Mark 4). Sift the flour, baking powder and cinnamon together and place in a mixing bowl with the sugar.

Beat together the eggs, milk and a pinch of salt. Pour the mixture into the center of the flour mixture and quickly mix together. Stir in the melted butter.

Pour the batter into a buttered and floured rectangular cake pan. Bake for 30 minutes and let cool before unmolding.

Meanwhile, melt the chocolate in a double boiler or in the microwave and let cool slightly.

Beat the whipping cream to stiff peaks and fold it into the cooled chocolate.

Slice the cake into rectangular pieces and frost them with the chocolate glaze. Let the glaze harden for a few minutes and then serve the cakes with a sprinkling of ground cinnamon if desired.

Preparation time **40 minutes**

Cooking time **35 minutes**

Level **medium**

citron and chocolate cake
with white chocolate sauce

Ingredients for 8 servings

Cake:

9 tbsps (4½ oz or 125 g) butter,
at room temperature

1 cup plus 2 tbsps (8 oz or 230 g) sugar

2 eggs, salt, **1/2** tsp baking powder

1½ cups (6½ oz or 185)
all-purpose flour

1/2 cup (1½ oz or 40 g) cocoa powder

3/4 cup (185 ml) milk

4 oz (120 g) dried figs, diced

2 oz (60 g) candied citron, diced

Sauce:

3½ oz (100 g) white chocolate

3 tbsps (50 ml) whipping cream

grated nutmeg

⌐ For an elegant variation,
replace the nutmeg with
a few pecan halves.

Preheat the oven to 350°F (180°C or Gas Mark 4).
Cream 8 tablespoons (4 oz or 120 g) of room
temperature butter and the sugar in a mixer until
the mixture is pale and fluffy.
Add the eggs one at a time and then a pinch of salt.
Sift together the flour, baking powder and cocoa powder.
Add a little of the flour mixture and then a little
of the milk. Continue until the milk and flour mixture
are all incorporated. Add the figs to the batter.
Butter a rectangular loaf pan and place a strip
of parchment paper along the bottom.
Pour the batter into the pan and smooth the top.
Sprinkle over the candied citron and bake for 45 minutes.
Meanwhile heat the whipping cream to a simmer
and add the chocolate. Remove from heat and stir until
the chocolate is melted, whisking to create a smooth
cream. Unmold the cake and let cool on a wire rack.
Slice and serve with the white chocolate sauce
and a little freshly grated nutmeg.

Preparation time **30 minutes**
Cooking time **50 minutes**
Level **medium**

milk chocolate sabayon tart
with caramelized strawberries

Ingredients for 8 servings
Tart:
9 tbsps (4½ oz or 125 g)
butter, softened
3 tbsps sugar
1 tsp vanilla extract, **1** egg, salt
1⅔ cups (7 oz or 200 g)
all-purpose flour
Sabayon:
9 oz (250 g) milk chocolate
2 eggs, **4** egg yolks, **3** tbsps sugar
3/4 cup (7 oz or 200 g) butter
Decoration:
3½ oz (100 g) strawberries, halved
2 tbsps raw cane sugar
1/2 cup (120 ml) whipping
cream, whipped
dark chocolate, shaved

Preheat the oven to 350°F (180°C or Gas Mark 4).
Make the tart: Cream the softened butter with the sugar
and vanilla. Add the egg, a pinch of salt and the flour. When the
dough is smooth form it into a ball and cover with plastic wrap.
Place in the refrigerator. Meanwhile, butter and flour
2 small- to medium-sized fluted tart tins. Roll out the dough
and line the tart tins with it. Place a sheet of parchment paper
over the tarts and fill with dried beans. Bake for 8 minutes,
remove the paper and weights and continue baking for another
5 minutes. Make the sabayon: Melt the milk chocolate over
a double boiler. In a round-bottomed pan beat the eggs and egg
yolks with the sugar. Place the pan over the already hot water
used for the chocolate and continue whisking until quadrupled
in volume. Stir the butter into the melted chocolate and then
whisk the mixture into the egg mixture. Remove from the heat
and pour the sabayon into the tart crusts. Bake the tarts
for 10 minutes. Remove from the oven, let cool and refrigerate.
Place the strawberries in a frying pan and sprinkle with the
sugar. Cook over medium heat until the sugar begins to
caramelize. Top the tarts with the strawberries, a dollop
of whipped cream and the chocolate shavings.

Adding 1/2 teaspoon cornstarch to the
sabayon will ensure that it doesn't
fall or separate while cooking.

Preparation time **30 minutes**
Cooking time **30 minutes**
Level **medium**

carrot and pistachio cake with white chocolate-limoncello frosting

Ingredients for 8 servings

Cake:

5½ oz (150 g) unsalted pistachios

3/4 cup (5½ oz or 150 g) sugar

grated zest of 1 organic lemon

5 medium carrots, peeled

4 eggs, salt

1/3 cup (1½ oz or 40 g) all-purpose flour

1 tsp baking powder

Frosting:

3½ oz (100 g) white chocolate

1 tbsp butter

grated zest of 1 organic lemon

1 tbsp limoncello liqueur

Preheat the oven to 320°F (160°C or Gas Mark 3). Finely grind the pistachios with the sugar and the zest of 1 lemon in a food processor. Transfer to a mixing bowl. Slice the carrots into rounds and then puree them in a food processor or blender with the eggs and a pinch of salt. Add the carrot mixture to the pistachio mixture and stir to combine. Sift in the flour and baking powder. Pour the batter into a 9-inch (22 cm) cake pan and bake for 10 minutes. Raise the oven temperature to 350°F (180°C or Gas Mark 4) and bake for another 35 minutes. Remove from the oven and cool on a wire rack. Meanwhile, melt the white chocolate and butter over a double boiler or in the microwave. Add the lemon zest. When the cake is completely cooled, add the limoncello to the chocolate mixture and stir to combine. Pour the frosting over the cake and spread evenly with a spatula. Let the frosting set in the refrigerator before serving.

Cakes

The frosting may be prepared with the juice of ½ lemon in place of the limoncello.

Preparation time **30 minutes**
Cooking time **45 minutes**
Level **easy**

milk chocolate and almond pavé

Ingredients for 8 servings

Pavé:

1 cup (5½ oz or 150 g) peeled almonds

2 oz (50 g) brioche bread

7 oz (200 g) milk chocolate

3½ oz (100 g) dark chocolate

2 tbsps brandy

10 tbsps (5½ oz or 150 g) butter, softened

3/4 cup (5½ oz or 150 g) sugar

4 eggs, lightly beaten

1 tsp vanilla extract

7 oz (200 g) mascarpone

Decoration:

cocoa powder, whipped cream (optional)

Preheat the oven to 325°F (170°C or Gas Mark 3).
Toast the almonds in the oven until they begin to brown.
Let cool and then finely grind in a food processor
together with the brioche.
Butter two 4-inch (10 cm) round cake pans and lightly
dust them with the ground almond mixture,
reserving any extra.
Melt the chocolate in the microwave. Add the brandy
and mix well. Let cool until the chocolate begins
to thicken. Cream the softened butter with the sugar.
Add the chocolate, beaten eggs, vanilla extract
and mascarpone. Add the remaining almond mixture
and pour the batter into the prepared pans.
Bake for 30 minutes. Let cool for 10 minutes before
unmolding. Dust the cakes with cocoa powder and
serve with whipped cream, if desired.

The brioche may be substituted
with leftover panettone, pandoro
or the Easter cake colomba.

Preparation time **35 minutes**
Cooking time **40 minutes**
Level **easy**

carrot and walnut cake
with chocolate frosting

Ingredients for 8 servings

Cake:

3 tbsps sunflower oil

5 eggs

3/4 cup (5½ oz or 150 g) sugar

1¼ cups (5½ oz or 150 g)
all-purpose flour

1/2 cup (1½ oz or 40 g) cocoa powder

2 large carrots, peeled and grated

1/3 cup plus 1 tbsp (2 oz or 50 g)
chopped walnuts

Frosting:

12½ oz (350 g) mascarpone

1¾ cups (6 oz or 175 g)
confectioners' sugar

6 oz (175 g) milk chocolate

Preheat the oven to 350°F (180°C or Gas Mark 4).
Oil an 8-inch (20 cm) cake pan and line with parchment
paper. Beat the eggs with the sugar over a double boiler.
Cook the mixture, stirring constantly, until it thickens,
forming a dense cream. Remove from heat and sift
in the flour and cocoa powder. Add the carrots, walnuts
and sunflower oil and mix well.
Pour the batter into the prepared cake pan and bake
for 45 minutes. Remove from the oven and cool completely
on a wire rack. Meanwhile, mix the mascarpone with
the confectioners' sugar.
Melt the chocolate over a double boiler or the microwave,
then let cool until tepid. Stir the chocolate into the
mascarpone mixture. Slice the cake in half horizontally.
Frost the bottom layer, cover with the top layer and frost
the top as well. Refrigerate for 20 minutes before serving.

For a delicious variation,
substitute the walnuts with the
same quantity of almonds and
proceed with the recipe.

Preparation time **30 minutes**
Cooking time **45 minutes**
Level **easy**

chocolate-glazed carrot cake
with almonds and coconut

Ingredients for 4 servings

Cake:

5 medium carrots, peeled

1 cup (5½ oz or 150 g) almonds

3/4 cup (5½ oz or 150 g) sugar

1¼ cups (5½ oz or 150 g) shredded coconut

3 eggs

1 tsp baking powder

Glaze:

7 oz (200 g) milk chocolate

shredded coconut (optional)

Preheat the oven to 320°F (160°C or Gas Mark 3).
Puree the carrots in a food processor and transfer
to a mixing bowl.
Grind the almonds with the sugar in a food processor
and add them to the carrots. Stir in the shredded coconut,
eggs and baking powder.
Stir with a wooden spoon to combine.
Pour the mixture into a 10-inch (24 cm) cake pan and bake
for 10 minutes. Raise the oven temperature to 350°F
(180°C or Gas Mark 4) and continue baking for 40 minutes.
Remove from the oven and let cool completely.
Meanwhile, melt the chocolate over a double boiler.
Pour the glaze over the cake, smoothing with a spatula.
Let the glaze harden before serving and decorate,
if desired, with shredded coconut.

Cakes

This cake may also be made in
a loaf pan. Due to its low fat
content, this is an ideal
breakfast cake.

Preparation time **30 minutes**
Cooking time **50 minutes**
Level **easy**

gianduia and ricotta tart

Ingredients for 8 servings
Crust:

3/4 cup (7 oz or 200 g) butter

1 cup (7 oz or 200 g) sugar

3¼ cups (14 oz or 400 g) all-purpose flour

2 eggs, **1** tsp vanilla extract, salt

Filling:

2 cups (500 ml) milk, **4** egg yolks

2/3 cup (4½ oz or 125 g) sugar

1/3 cup plus 1 tbsp (2 oz or 50 g) all-purpose flour

3 drops hazelnut extract

3 oz (80 g) gianduia chocolate, chopped

3½ oz (100 g) fresh ricotta

Mix together the ingredients for the crust.
When the dough comes together, knead it with the palm of the hand for a few minutes and then form into a disk. Cover with plastic wrap and refrigerate.
Preheat the oven to 350°F (180°C or Gas Mark 4)
Heat the milk in a saucepan over low heat. Beat the eggs and sugar in a mixing bowl and stir in the flour and hazelnut extract. Whisk the boiling hot milk into the egg mixture and return to the saucepan. Cook over low heat, stirring with a whisk, until the cream thickens. Remove from the heat and add the chocolate.
Stir until the chocolate is melted and the cream is smooth. Let cool and then stir in the ricotta.
Roll out three-quarters of the dough on a lightly floured work surface. Butter and flour a tart pan and line it with the dough. Pierce the dough with a fork and fill with the gianduia-ricotta mixture. Roll out the remaining dough and cut it into strips. Make a criss-cross lattice over the top of the tart. Bake for about 30 minutes.
Let cool and refrigerate for 1 hour before serving.

Preparation time **40 minutes**
Cooking time **40 minutes**
Level **easy**

Cakes

250

Gianduia is made from a mixture of chocolate and hazelnuts and is originally from the northeastern Italian region of Piedmont, known for its hazelnuts.

carrot, chocolate and coconut cake

Ingredients for 4 servings

Cake:

3 eggs, **5** tbsps sunflower oil

1⅔ cups (7 oz or 200 g)
all-purpose flour

3/4 cups (3½ oz or 100 g)
shredded coconut

3/4 cups (5½ oz or 150 g) sugar

3 tbsps milk, **2** tsps vanilla extract

3/4 cups (5½ oz or 150 g)
grated carrots

1 tsp baking powder

3½ oz (100 g) coconut-flavored
chocolate, chopped

Preheat the oven to 350°F (180°C or Gas Mark 4).
Mix together the eggs, flour, shredded coconut, sugar,
sunflower oil, milk, vanilla, grated carrots and baking
powder.
Pour the batter into a buttered and floured cake pan.
Add the chocolate pieces and stir in with a wooden spoon.
Bake for 30 minutes.
Serve warm, decorated, if desired with confectioners'
sugar and shredded coconut.

Cakes

252

For best results, spread the grated
carrots in an even layer over a clean
kitchen towel. Cover with another
towel and let dry for about 1 hour.

Preparation time **20 minutes**
Cooking time **30 minutes**
Level **easy**

ricotta tart with gianduiotti

Ingredients for 8 servings

Crust:

2⅓ cups plus 1 tbsp (10½ oz or 300 g) all purpose flour

1/2 cup (3½ oz or 100 g) confectioner's sugar

3/4 cup (7 oz or 200 g) butter

1 egg yolk, grated zest from 1 lemon, salt

Filling:

1 handful raisins, **14** oz (400 g) fresh ricotta

1/4 cup (1 oz or 30 g) all-purpose flour

2 eggs, **1/3** cup (2½ oz or 70 g) sugar

ground cinnamon

20 gianduiotti (see note), chopped

⌐ Gianduiotti are small triangular chocolates made from a mixture of hazelnut and chocolate. They can be replaced with 7 oz (200 g) gianduia chocolate, or 4 oz (120 g) coffee-flavored chocolate.

Mix together the ingredients for the crust. When the dough comes together form it into a disk and cover with plastic wrap. Refrigerate for 1 hour.
Preheat the oven to 325°F (170°C or Gas Mark 3).
Roll out three-quarters of the dough. Butter and flour a spring-form pan and line it with the dough.
Roll the raisins in the flour.
Beat the eggs and sugar with an electric mixer until thick and pale yellow. Add the ricotta and a pinch of ground cinnamon and mix well. Stir the raisins and chopped gianduiotti into the cream with a wooden spoon.
Pierce the crust with a fork and pour in the filling.
Roll out the remaining dough and cut it into thin strips.
Decorate the top of the tart with the dough strips, forming a lattice, or any other desired pattern.
Bake for 35 minutes. Remove from the oven and let cool completely before removing from the pan.
Dust with confectioners' sugar if desired.

Preparation time **30 minutes**
Cooking time **35 minutes**
Level **easy**

Cakes

milk chocolate and almond cake

Ingredients for 8 servings

Cake:

3/4 cup (7 oz or 200 g) butter, at room temperature

1¼ cups (250 g) sugar

1 tsp vanilla extract

4 eggs, separated

1/2 cup (2 oz or 60 g) all-purpose flour

4 tbsps cocoa powder

2 tbsps cornstarch, salt

2½ cups (9 oz or 250 g) ground almonds

Frosting:

6 tbsps whipping cream

7 oz (200 g) milk chocolate, chopped

Preheat the oven to 350°F (180°C or Gas Mark 4).
Cream the butter with the sugar and vanilla.
Add the egg yolks one at a time. Sift in the flour, cocoa powder and cornstarch. Add the ground almonds and stir to combine. Beat the egg whites and a pinch of salt to stiff peaks and carefully fold them into the batter.
Butter and flour a spring-form pan and pour in the batter. Bake for 40 minutes. Remove the cake from the oven, let cool completely and unmold. Meanwhile, heat the cream and whisk in the chocolate, stirring until the cream is smooth and fluid. Let the frosting harden slightly. Frost the cooled cake and refrigerate for 20 minutes before serving.

If the frosting becomes too hard, beat it with a wooden spoon until it softens and reaches the correct consistency.

Preparation time **20 minutes**
Cooking time **40 minutes**
Level **easy**

chocolate-hazelnut cake with dates

Ingredients for 8 servings

Cake:

2/3 cup (3½ oz or 100 g) blanched hazelnuts

4 oz (120 g) milk chocolate

3 egg whites, salt

1¼ cup (4½ oz or 125 g) confectioners' sugar

3½ oz (120 g) pitted dates, finely chopped

1 pat of butter

Decoration:

1/2 cup (120 ml) whipping cream

1 tbsp confectioner's sugar

1/2 tsp vanilla extract

Preheat the oven to 350°F (180°C or Gas Mark 4).
Grind the hazelnuts and the milk chocolate together in a food processor.
Beat the egg whites and a pinch of salt to stiff peaks, adding the confectioner's sugar a little at a time.
Add the ground hazelnut and chocolate mixture and then the dates. Pour the batter into a buttered spring-form pan. Bake for 35 minutes, remove from the oven and let cool.
Unmold the meringue and slice in half horizontally. Whip the whipping cream with the confectioners' sugar and vanilla. Spread the whipped cream on half of the meringue and top with the other half. Serve immediately.

For best results, keep the whipping cream cold until ready to use.

Preparation time **30 minutes**
Cooking time **35 minutes**
Level **medium**

chocolate rum-raisin cake

Ingredients for 4 servings
Cake:

1 cup (4½ oz or 140 g) raisins
6 tbsps dark rum, **3** eggs, beaten
1½ cups (6½ oz or 185 g)
all-purpose flour
11 tbsps (5½ oz or 150 g)
melted butter
3/4 cup (4½ oz or 140 g) sugar
1/2 tsp baking powder
1/3 cup (2½ oz or 70 g)
chocolate chips
Decoration:
whipped cream or other pastry cream

 Serve this cake with this crème:
Beat 10 egg yolks with 1 3/4 cups (12½ oz
or 350 g) sugar until thick and creamy. Boil
2 cups (500 ml) milk with 1 vanilla bean.
Remove the bean and whisk the hot milk
into the egg mixture. Return to the heat
and continue cooking, whisking
constantly, until thickened.

Preheat the oven to 350°F (180°C or Gas Mark 4).
Soak the raisins in the rum for 15 minutes.
Sift the flour into a mixing bowl and form a hollow
in the middle. Add the melted butter and sugar.
Stir with a wooden spoon and then add the beaten eggs.
Add the baking powder and chocolate chips and stir
with a wooden spoon until smooth.
Line a cake pan with parchment paper and pour in the
batter. Smooth the surface with a spatula and bake
for 40 minutes.
Check to see if the cake is done by inserting a toothpick
into the center. If it comes out clean, remove the cake
from the oven. Let cool completely. Serve the cake with
whipped cream or other pastry cream.

Preparation time **20 minutes**
Cooking time **50 minutes**
Level **easy**

milk chocolate citrus cake

Ingredients for 4 servings
Cake:

5½ oz (150 g) milk chocolate

grated zest of **1** organic orange

grated zest of **1** organic lemon

1/2 cup (2 oz or 60 g) all-purpose flour

3/4 cup (3½ oz or 95 g) almonds

4 eggs, separated, **1/2** tsp baking powder

2/3 cup (4½ oz or 125 g) sugar

2 tbsps warm milk, salt

Decoration:

2/3 cup plus 1 tbsp (170 ml) whipping cream

confectioners' sugar

milk chocolate, shaved (optional)

Preheat the oven to 350°F (180°C or Gas Mark 4). Butter a spring-form pan and line the bottom with parchment paper. Pulse two-thirds of the chocolate in a food processor with the orange and lemon zest. Add the flour and almonds and pulse until blended. Using an electric mixer, beat the egg yolks with the sugar and add to the chocolate-almond mixture. Stir in the milk. Beat the egg whites with a pinch of salt and fold them into the batter. Carefully mix in the baking powder and pour the batter into the prepared pan. Bake for 45 minutes, remove from the oven and cool completely. Slice the cake in half horizontally. Whip the whipping cream and use it to frost the bottom layer of the cake. Cover with the top layer and refrigerate for 20 minutes. Dust with confectioner's sugar and decorate with milk chocolate shavings if desired.

Cakes

262

This cake may be filled with orange marmalade instead of whipped cream and topped with toasted slivered almonds.

Preparation time **30 minutes**
Cooking time **45 minutes**
Level **medium**

chocolate-vanilla marbled bundt cake

Ingredients for 4 servings

Bundt Cake:

12 tbsps (6 oz or 175 g) butter

2/3 cup (4½ oz or 130 g) sugar

1 tsp vanilla extract

3 eggs

1¾ cups (8 oz or 225 g) all-purpose flour

salt

1/2 tsp baking powder

2 oz (50 g) milk chocolate

Preheat the oven to 375°F (190°C or Gas Mark 5).
Cream the butter and sugar together. Add the vanilla and then the eggs.
Sift in the flour, a pinch of salt and the baking powder.
Transfer half of the batter to another bowl.
Melt the chocolate over a double boiler or the microwave. Let cool slightly, and when tepid add it to half of the batter. Stir until the color is uniform.
Butter a medium-sized Bundt pan.
Fill the pan with spoonfuls of the batter, alternating chocolate and plain batter. Bake the cake for 30 minutes. Let cool and unmold before serving.
This cake makes a good accompaniment to a cup of tea.

This cake can be served with Mascarpone cream: Whip together 3½ oz. mascarpone, 4 tbsp sugar, 1 tbsp Rum, and 2 egg yolks. Beat the egg whites to stiff peaks and fold into the cream.

Preparation time **20 minutes**
Cooking time **30 minutes**
Level **easy**

gianduia mousse tart

Ingredients for 8 servings
Crust:

3/4 cup (2 oz or 60 g) ground hazelnuts

1⅓ cups (5½ oz or 165 g)
all-purpose flour

2 tbsps (1 oz or 30 g) sugar

9 tbsps (4½ oz or 125 g) butter, **1** egg

Mousse:

4½ oz (125 g) gianduia chocolate

4 tbsps (2 oz or 50 g) butter, **2** eggs

7 tbsps (3½ oz or 100 g) sugar

2 tbsps all-purpose flour

4 tbsps whipping cream

1 tbsp brandy

The same quantity of ground almonds may be used in place of the hazelnuts in the crust. The gianduia chocolate may be substituted with milk chocolate or coffee-flavored chocolate.

Mix together the ground hazelnuts, flour and sugar. Add the butter and work with the fingertips until the mixture resembles a coarse meal. Beat the egg with a little water and add just enough to form a smooth dough. Form into a disk, wrap in plastic wrap and refrigerate for 30 minutes. Preheat the oven to 350°F (180°C or Gas Mark 4).
Roll out the dough on a lightly floured work surface. Butter and flour a round tart tin and line it with the dough. Pierce the dough with a fork and cover with waxed paper. Place pie weights or dried beans on the paper and bake for 12-13 minutes in the bottom half of the oven.
Meanwhile, melt the chocolate and butter over a double boiler, remove from heat and let cool.
Beat the eggs and the sugar for 10 minutes, until thick and creamy.
Sift in the flour and stir in the cooled chocolate mixture. Add the cream and brandy and mix well.
Pour the filling into the tart crust and bake for another 15 minutes. Let cool on a wire rack, then serve.

Preparation time **30 minutes**
Cooking time **30 minutes**
Level **medium**

lemon tart with blueberries and white chocolate

Ingredients for 8 servings

Tart:

9 oz (350 g) shortcrust dough (see p. 386)

3 eggs

2/3 cup (4½ oz or 125 g) sugar

4 tbsps whipping cream

2 organic lemons

1 tbsp cornstarch

Topping:

2 oz (50 g) white chocolate

2 tbsps whipping cream

1 basket of blueberries

Preheat the oven to 350°F (180°C or Gas Mark 4). Roll out the shortcrust dough on a lightly floured work surface. Butter and flour a tart tin and line it with the dough. Pierce the bottom of the dough with a fork and refrigerate for 20 minutes.

Place a sheet of aluminum foil over the dough and cover with dried beans or pie weights. Bake for 10 minutes. Remove from the oven and cool completely.

Using an electric mixer, beat the eggs with the sugar, the juice of 1 lemon and the grated zest from both lemons. Add the whipping cream and cornstarch and continue beating until thick.

Pour the filling into the cooled tart crust and bake for 15 minutes. Lower the oven temperature to 320°F (160°C) or Gas Mark 3) and bake for another 20 minutes. Remove from the oven and let cool.

Meanwhile, melt the white chocolate, stir in the whipping cream, and spread the mixture over the top of the tart. Top with the blueberries and serve.

Cakes

268

Cornstarch is a thickening agent used to flour foods before cooking or to thicken sauces and creams. Potato starch may be used in place of cornstarch.

Preparation time **30 minutes**
Cooking time **35 minutes**
Level **medium**

pandoro and gianduia tart

Ingredients for 6 servings

Crust:

2⅓ cups plus 1 tbsp (10½ oz or 300 g) all-purpose flour

12 tbsps (6 oz or 170 g) butter

3/4 cup (5½ oz or 150 g) sugar

1 egg plus 1 egg yolk

1 tsp vanilla extract

salt

Filling:

4 oz (120 g) gianduia chocolate, chopped

4 tbsps whipping cream

6½ oz (180 g) pandoro

Place the flour into a bowl and make a well at the center. Place the butter, sugar, egg, egg yolk, vanilla and a pinch of salt in the center.
Quickly mix with fingertips to form a smooth dough.
Wrap in plastic wrap and refrigerate for 40 minutes.
Preheat the oven to 325°F (170°C or Gas Mark 3).
Butter and flour a round tart pan.
Roll out the dough on a lightly floured work surface.
Line the prepared pan with the dough. Pierce the dough with a fork and cover with parchment paper. Cover with dried beans or pie weights and bake for 20 minutes.
The crust should be cooked but not colored or dry.
Remove from the oven and let cool.
Meanwhile, melt the gianduia chocolate over a double boiler or in the microwave. Let cool slightly.
Whip the whipping cream, fold it into the chocolate and crumble in the pandoro.
Fill the cooked crust with the chocolate filling.
Serve immediately.

Cakes

For a crunchier version of this tart, replace the pandoro with 7 oz (200 g) crumbled amaretto cookies.

Preparation time **30 minutes**
Cooking time **25 minutes**
Level **easy**

milk and white chocolate desserts

chocolate

milk chocolate mousse

Ingredients for 6 servings

Mousse:

5½ oz (150 g) milk chocolate

3 tbsps sugar

8 tbsps water

2 egg whites

1½ gelatin sheets

2 tbsps instant coffee

1¾ cups (400 ml) whipping cream

The secret to a perfect mousse is its lightness. It is important to add the ingredients to the egg whites gradually and in small quantities. Make sure to use a gentle folding technique when incorporating ingredients into the egg whites, being careful not to lose the airy consistency

Shave a few spoonfuls of chocolate and set aside. Roughly chop the remaining chocolate. Heat the sugar in a small saucepan with 6 tablespoons water and cook until the liquid becomes thick and syrupy. When the syrup comes to a boil, remove from heat and set aside. Beat the egg whites until they begin to form peaks. Slowly pour the sugar syrup into the egg whites, beating continuously, until all of the syrup has been incorporated. Continue to beat the egg whites until the mixture has cooled and the whites form stiff peaks. Soak the gelatin sheets in cold water. Meanwhile, melt the chocolate over a double boiler or in the microwave. Heat the remaining 2 tablespoons water and add the instant coffee. Stir to dissolve. Drain the gelatin sheets and squeeze out the excess water. Add to the coffee and stir to dissolve. Add the coffee mixture to the egg whites and then fold in the melted chocolate. Whip the cream and fold it into the chocolate mixture. Spoon the mousse into 6 coffee or tea cups. Cover with plastic wrap and refrigerate for 1 hour. Top the mousse with the reserved chocolate shavings and serve.

Preparation time **20 minutes**
Cooking time **5 minutes**
Level **easy**

coconut granita with milk chocolate sauce

Ingredients for 4 servings

Granita:

1¾ cups (400 ml) sweetened coconut milk

2⅔ cups (9 oz or 250 g) shaved fresh coconut meat

Sauce:

3 oz (80 g) milk chocolate

3 tbsps whipping cream

Pour the coconut milk into a large stainless-steel bowl and freeze for at least 2 hours, beating it with an electric mixer every 30 minutes.
Meanwhile, melt the chocolate with the cream over a double boiler or in the microwave. Stir the mixture until cooled. Pour the chocolate sauce in the bottom of 4 glasses, sprinkle over the shaved coconut and top with the granita.

Instead of stirring the granita with a mixer every 30 minutes it may be left in the freezer for the full 2 hours and then blended just before serving.

Preparation time **15 minutes**
Cooking time **5 minutes**
Level **easy**

milk chocolate pots de crème

Ingredients for 6 servings
Pots de crème:

1/2 vanilla bean, halved lengthwise

1½ cups plus 2 tbsps (375 ml) milk

2½ oz (70 g) milk chocolate, chopped

2/3 cups (150 ml) whipping cream

3 egg yolks

1/2 cup (3½ oz or 100 g) sugar

Decoration:

4 tbsps cocoa powder

whipped cream

1 oz (30 g) dark chocolate, shaved

Preheat the oven to 325°F (170°C or Gas Mark 3).
Place the vanilla bean in a saucepan with the milk.
Bring to a simmer and remove from heat.
Let the milk infuse for 10 minutes and then remove
the vanilla bean. Add the chocolate and then the cream.
Stir until the chocolate is melted and set aside.
Beat the egg yolks with the sugar until thick and pale
yellow. Slowly whisk the chocolate mixture into the eggs.
Pour the chocolate cream into 6 ramequins and place
them in a baking dish.
Fill the baking dish half full of hot water and bake
for 30 minutes, or until the cream has just set.
Let the pots de crème cool and then decorate with cocoa
powder, whipped cream and chocolate shavings.

For an even prettier presentation,
use heat-resistant glass
cups in place of ramequins.

Preparation time **30 minutes**
Cooking time **30 minutes**
Level **easy**

white chocolate mousse with lemon jelly

Ingredients for 8 servings

Mousse:

9 oz (250 g) white chocolate, chopped

2 egg whites

salt

2/3 cup (150 ml) whipping cream

2 gelatin sheets

grated zest and juice from
1 organic lemon

Lemon Jelly:

juice of 2 organic lemons

3 tbsps water

1 tbsp sugar

1 tsp agar agar or 1 gelatin sheet

This delicate mousse is an ideal summer dessert. Try serving it with seasonal mixed berries.

Melt the white chocolate over a double boiler or in the microwave. Beat the egg whites and a pinch of salt to stiff peaks. Then beat the whipping cream to stiff peaks and set aside.

Soak the gelatin in cold water for a few minutes, drain and squeeze out the excess water. Meanwhile, mix together the lemon zest and 5 tablespoons lemon juice. Heat the mixture slightly and then add the gelatin sheets. Pour the white chocolate over the whipped cream and fold together. Let cool and then add the lemon juice mixture. Carefully fold in the egg whites, making gentle movements from the top to the bottom of the mixture.

Transfer the mixture to a large bowl, cover with plastic wrap and refrigerate until firm.

Meanwhile make the jelly: Mix together the lemon juice, water and sugar in a small saucepan.

Briefly heat the mixture and add the agar agar or the soaked gelatin sheet. Strain the mixture and pour into silicon jelly molds. Refrigerate until firm.

Unmold the jellies and roughly chop them. Serve the white chocolate mousse with a spoonful of lemon jelly.

Preparation time **25 minutes**
Cooking time **10 minutes**
Level **medium**

coffee bavarian creams
with two chocolate sauces

Desserts

Ingredients for 6 servings

Bavarian creams:

6 gelatin sheets, **2** cups (500 ml) milk

10 coffee beans, **4** egg yolks

3/4 cups (5½ oz or 150 g) sugar

1/2 cup (120 ml) prepared espresso coffee

7 tbsps whipping cream

1/4 cup (60 ml) brandy

Sauces:

3½ oz (100 g) white chocolate, shaved

3½ oz (100 g) dark chocolate, shaved

7 tbsps whipping cream

1 tbsp instant coffee

Soak the gelatin sheets in cold water for a few minutes. Meanwhile, bring the milk and coffee beans to a boil. Strain the milk and set aside.

Beat the egg yolks with the sugar until thick. Whisk in the hot milk and the espresso coffee.

Transfer the mixture to a saucepan and heat over low heat, stirring constantly. Continue cooking the mixture until it coats the back of a wooden spoon and begins to thicken. Drain the gelatin, squeeze out the excess water and stir into the coffee mixture.

Whip the whipping cream and fold it into the mixture. Coat individual ramekins or the inside of a Bundt pan with the brandy and pour in the coffee cream.

Refrigerate for 4-5 hours.

Make the sauces: Melt the two types of chocolate separately, adding half of the cream to each.

Stir until the chocolate is melted and the cream has been incorporated. Sprinkle the coffee Bavarian creams with instant coffee and serve with the two chocolate sauces.

282 ⌐ For best results in unmolding the creams, place the bottom of the mold in hot water for a few minutes just before serving. Remove from the water, dry the mold and carefully invert onto a serving plate.

Preparation time **20 minutes**
Cooking time **15 minutes**
Level **easy**

jasmine-infused white chocolate cream

Ingredients for 4 servings

Cream:

3 gelatin sheets

1 cup (250 ml) milk

2 oz (60 g) jasmine flowers

salt

1 vanilla bean, halved lengthwise

3 egg yolks

1/4 cup (2 oz or 50 g) sugar

3½ oz (100 g) white chocolate, shaved

1¼ cups (300 ml) whipping cream

Sauce:

7 tbsps (100 ml) milk

1/4 cup (2 oz or 50 g) sugar

mint syrup

Decoration:

fresh jasmine flowers

Soak the gelatin sheets in cold water for a few minutes.
Bring the milk to a boil with the jasmine flowers,
a pinch of salt and the vanilla bean.
Remove from heat and set aside to infuse.
Meanwhile, beat the egg yolks with the sugar until thick
and pale yellow. Whisk the hot milk infusion into the egg
yolks and stir until the mixture coats the back of a spoon.
Strain the mixture and add the white chocolate shavings.
Drain the gelatin, squeeze out the excess water and add
to the white chocolate cream. Stir until the chocolate
is melted and the gelatin incorporated, then set aside
to cool. Whip the whipping cream to stiff peaks
and fold it into the cooled white chocolate cream.
Pour into a mold and refrigerate until cool.
Meanwhile make the sauce: Bring the milk and sugar
to a boil. Remove from heat and stir in the mint syrup.
Let cool. Serve the white chocolate cream with the mint
sauce and decorate with fresh jasmine flowers.

Preparation time **25 minutes**
Cooking time **10 minutes**
Level **easy**

bavarian cream with raspberries

Ingredients for 4 servings
Bavarian Cream:

3/4 cup plus 1 tbsp (200 ml) milk
1 vanilla bean, halved lengthwise
6 oz (170 g) white chocolate
2 gelatin sheets
2 egg yolks
3/4 cup (5½ or 150 g) sugar
1 cup (250 ml) whipping cream
1 basket of raspberries

Heat the milk and vanilla bean. Let cool slightly, scrape the vanilla seeds out of the bean and add them to the milk. Discard the bean. Chop the chocolate and melt it in the warm milk. Soak the gelatin in cold water. Drain, squeeze out the excess water and add the milk and chocolate. Stir to dissolve the gelatin.
Beat the egg yolks with the sugar until thick and creamy. Whisk the warm milk mixture into the eggs and let cool. Whip the whipping cream to stiff peaks and fold into the chocolate cream. Fold in the raspberries. Line a loaf pan with plastic wrap and pour the cream into the pan. Refrigerate for at least 3 hours. Slice and serve.

Bavarian cream is also known as crème bavaroise, or bavarois, thought to have been invented in Switzerland.

Preparation time **20 minutes**
Cooking time **15 minutes**
Level **easy**

milk chocolate-rum pudding

Ingredients for 6 servings

Pudding:

1¼ cups (300 ml) milk

3/4 cup plus 1 tbsp (200 ml) whipping cream

7 oz (200 g) milk chocolate, chopped

3 egg yolks

1/3 cup plus 2 tbsps (3 oz or 80 g) sugar

1 tbsp aged rum

1/3 cup (1 oz or 25 g) cocoa powder

3 gelatin sheets

Bring the milk and cream to a boil in a small saucepan, remove from heat and stir in the chocolate.
Beat the egg yolks with the sugar until thick and pale yellow. Add the rum and cocoa powder and set aside.
Soak the gelatin in cold water for a few minutes.
Drain and squeeze out the excess liquid.
Add the gelatin to the chocolate mixture.
When cool, whisk the egg yolks into the chocolate mixture.
Line a rectangular loaf pan with plastic wrap and pour in the chocolate cream. Refrigerate for at least 1 hour.
Unmold and serve.

This pudding may be served with whipped cream, a sweet sauce such as crème anglais or sabayon, or a fruit compote spiked with a liqueur of choice.

Preparation time **30 minutes**
Cooking time **15 minutes**
Level **easy**

creamy spiced hot chocolate

Ingredients for 4 servings
Hot Chocolate:

2 cups (500 ml) milk

1 cinnamon stick

2 star anise

1/2 vanilla bean, sliced lengthwise

1/4 cup (1 oz or 30 g) slivered almonds, toasted

3½ oz (100 g) milk chocolate, finely chopped

Heat the milk in a small saucepan with the cinnamon stick, star anise and vanilla bean.
Just as it starts to simmer add the almonds.
Remove from heat before it comes to a boil, then let sit for 10-15 minutes.
Strain the milk infusion, add the chocolate and return to heat. Whisk until the chocolate is completely melted.
Serve hot in porcelain tea cups or demi-tasse cups.

Complete this spiced hot chocolate with a dollop of whipped cream before serving. A pinch of freshly ground nutmeg enhances the spicy flavor of the hot chocolate.

Preparation time **5 minutes**
Cooking time **10 minutes**
Level **easy**

blackberry cake with milk chocolate sauce

Ingredients for 4 servings

Cake:

1 basket of blackberries, **2** tbsps sugar

2/3 cup (150 ml) water

4 sponge cake rounds (see p. 386)

5½ oz (150 g) mascarpone

5½ oz (150 g) ricotta

2 tbsps confectioners' sugar

grated zest of **1** lemon

1 tsp vanilla extract

1/4 cup (60 ml) whipping cream

Chocolate sauce:

3½ oz (100 g) milk chocolate

1/4 cup (60 ml) whipping cream

Garnish:

20 blackberries

Brioche may be used instead
of sponge cake for the base
of this dessert.

Place the blackberries in a saucepan with the sugar
and water. Bring to a boil and cook for 8 minutes.
Remove from the heat and puree in a food processor.
Slice each sponge cake round in half horizontally.
Brush the 8 sponge cake rounds with the berry puree.
Whip the mascarpone and ricotta with the confectioners'
sugar, lemon zest and vanilla extract.
Whip the whipping cream to stiff peaks and fold into
the mascarpone mixture.
Fill a pastry bag with the mascarpone filling.
Pipe the filling between each layer, finishing
with a layer of filling. Decorate with blackberries.
Heat the chocolate and whipping cream over a double
boiler. Stir until melted and remove from heat.
Serve with the chocolate sauce.

Preparation time **25 minutes**
Cooking time **10 minutes**
Level **easy**

blackberry ice cream with chocolate sauce and almond brittle

Ingredients for 4 servings

Brittle:

5 tbsps sugar

1/4 cup (1 oz or 30 g) slivered almonds

Ice cream:

7 oz (200 g) blackberry ice cream

Sauce:

2 tbsps cocoa powder

2 tbsps milk

1/4 cup (60 ml) whipping cream

3½ oz (100 g) white chocolate

Heat the sugar with a little water in a small saucepan. Cook without stirring until the sugar begins to caramelize. Meanwhile, toast the almonds and spread them in a single layer onto a piece of parchment paper.
Pour the caramel over the almonds and spread into an even layer with a spatula. Let sit until hardened.
Whisk the cocoa powder and the milk together in a small saucepan to form a smooth paste.
Whisk in the cream and add the white chocolate.
Heat the mixture, stirring constantly, until the chocolate has melted and the sauce is smooth.
Pour the warm sauce into 4 glass bowls or cups, balance the almond brittle on top and then top with a scoop of blackberry ice cream. Serve immediately

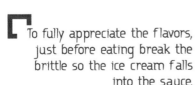
To fully appreciate the flavors, just before eating break the brittle so the ice cream falls into the sauce.

Preparation time **20 minutes**
Cooking time **10 minutes**
Level **easy**

coffee cream millefueilles

Ingredients for 4 servings

Pastry:

14 oz (400 g) shortcrust pastry crust (see p. 386)

Coffee cream:

5 oz (140 g) gianduia chocolate

4 oz (130 g) dark chocolate

2 tbsps instant coffee

1 cup plus 1 tbsp (280 ml) whipping cream

Decoration:

vanilla sugar

1 vanilla bean

Preheat the oven to 350°F (180°C or Gas Mark 4). Place both types of chocolate, the coffee and 1/3 cup (80 ml) of the whipping cream over a double boiler and heat until the chocolate is melted.
Remove from heat and cool slightly
Meanwhile, roll out the pastry into a thin sheet and cut it into 12 rectangles. Bake the pastry rectangles for 12 minutes. Remove from the oven and cool completely.
Beat the remaining whipping cream into stiff peaks and slowly drizzle over the chocolate mixture. Carefully fold the chocolate into the whipped cream. Transfer the chocolate cream to a pastry bag with a ridged tip.
Pipe 3 puffs of cream onto 4 pastry rectangles and top with more pastry rectangles. Repeat until the pastry is finished, creating a three-layered millefeuille.
Dust the millefeuilles with vanilla sugar and decorate with vanilla bean. Serve immediately.

Substitute the dark chocolate with a rum-infused chocolate for a stronger flavored chocolate cream.

Preparation time **20 minutes**
Cooking time **30 minutes**
Level **easy**

white chocolate-coconut mousse

Ingredients for 8 servings

Mousse:

9 oz (250 g) white chocolate

2 gelatin sheets

3½ tbsps coconut milk

5 tbsps coconut liqueur

7 tbsps whipping cream

2 egg whites

salt

grated zest from 1 organic lime

Melt the white chocolate over a double boiler or in the microwave, remove from the heat and cool until tepid.
Soak the gelatin in cold water for a few minutes.
Drain and squeeze out the excess water.
Dissolve the gelatin in the coconut milk and coconut liqueur and set aside.
Meanwhile, whip the whipping cream into stiff peaks.
Fold the melted chocolate into the whipped cream.
Add the coconut milk mixture to the whipped cream mixture and stir carefully incorporate.
Beat the egg whites and a pinch of salt to stiff peaks and fold into the coconut mixture.
Add the lime zest and transfer the mixture to a bowl.
Refrigerate until firm.

This mousse may also be made in a "dark" version. Substitute the white chocolate with top-quality dark chocolate, the coconut liqueur with dark rum and omit the lime zest.

Preparation time **20 minutes**
Cooking time **10 minutes**
Level **easy**

gianduia parfait with pear gratin and rum sauce

Ingredients for 4 servings

Parfait :

3½ oz (100 g) gianduia chocolate

1/3 cup (2 oz or 65 g) sugar

2 tbsps water

2 eggs, separated, **1** egg yolk

1 tsp instant coffee, **1** tbsp brandy

1/3 cup (80 ml) whipping cream

Gratin:

1 pear

3 tbsps raw cane sugar

Rum sauce:

1 cup (250 ml) milk

1/2 vanilla bean, sliced lengthwise

2 egg yolks

1/3 cup (2 oz or 65 g) sugar

1 tbsp rum

Slowly melt the chocolate over a double boiler. Meanwhile, bring the sugar and water to a boil over high heat and cook for 2 minutes. Beat the egg yolks until they begin to thicken then pour in the boiling sugar syrup in a thin stream, whisking constantly. Add the instant coffee and brandy. Set aside to cool. Beat the whipping cream to stiff peaks. Fold the melted chocolate into the cooled egg yolk mixture, making sure that the two mixtures are about the same temperature. Fold in the whipped cream and transfer the batter into individual aluminum ramequins. Freeze until set. Preheat the oven to 400°F (200°C or Gas Mark 6). Peel and quarter the pear. Slice each pear quarter into 4 layers, leaving the layers attached at the top to form a fan. Place the pear fans on a baking sheet, sprinkle with raw cane sugar and bake until the sugar is golden-brown and caramelized. Make the rum sauce: Heat the milk and vanilla bean in a saucepan. Beat the egg yolks and the sugar until thick. Strain the milk and whisk it into the egg yolks. Return to the saucepan and cook over low heat, stirring constantly until the cream has thickened and coats the back of a spoon. Add the rum and strain the cream using a chinois sieve. Place a spoonful of sauce on each plate and top with the unmolded gianduia parfait and the pear gratin.

Preparation time **30 minutes**
Cooking time **20 minutes**
Level **difficult**

white chocolate-coffee sauce

Ingredients for 4 servings

Sauce:

3 tbsps milk

1 tbsp Arabica coffee beans

7 tbsps whipping cream

3 oz (80 g) white chocolate

Heat the milk in a small saucepan, remove from heat and cool slightly.

Pour the milk into a bowl with the coffee beans and let sit long enough for the flavors to infuse but not to color the milk. Strain the mixture and refrigerate for 8 hours.

Heat the cream and the strained milk together.

Add the white chocolate and whisk until the chocolate is melted and the sauce is smooth and fluid.

Let cool completely and use to accompany semifreddos or other dark chocolate desserts.

This sauce pairs well with cakes like pandoro and panettone or any type of sponge cake.

Preparation time **20 minutes**
Cooking time **5 minutes**
Level **easy**

torrone semifreddo with gianduia sauce

Ingredients for 4 servings

Semifreddo:

4 eggs, separated

1/2 cup (3½ oz or 100 g) sugar

1¾ cups (400 ml) whipping cream

salt

5½ oz (150 g) hazelnut torrone (nougat), finely chopped

1/2 tsp instant coffee

Sauce:

2 tbsps whipping cream

2 oz (50 g) gianduia chocolate

Beat the egg yolks and sugar in a mixing bowl.
In another bowl, whip the whipping cream and then fold into the egg yolk mixture.
Beat the egg whites and a pinch of salt into stiff peaks and then fold into the eggs and cream.
Carefully fold in three-quarters of the torrone and the instant coffee. Line 4 ramequins with foil and pour in the semifreddo. Freeze for at least 3 hours.
Just before serving, heat the whipping cream and gianduia for the sauce until melted.
Unmold the semifreddos, drizzle with gianduia sauce and top with the remaining torrone.

An electric mixer is a useful kitchen appliance which can be used for blending, mixing and pureeing various types of preparations.

Preparation time **20 minutes**
Cooking time **5 minutes**
Level **easy**

milk chocolate mousse on strawberry tartare

Ingredients for 10 servings

Wafers:
1/2 cup (2½ oz or 70 g) all-purpose flour
5 tbsps (2½ oz or 70 g) butter
1/2 cup plus 1 tbsp (2½ oz or 70 g) confectioners' sugar
1/2 cup (2½ oz or 70 g) pistachios
2 egg whites

Mousse:
1 cup (8 oz or 225 g), **3** gelatin sheets crushed strawberries
3/4 cup (170 ml) crème anglais (see p. 300)
1⅓ lbs (600 g) milk chocolate
1¾ cups plus 1 tbsp (475 ml) whipping cream

Tartare:
1½ lbs (700 g) strawberries, hulled and diced
3/4 cup (5½ oz or 150 g) raw cane sugar, juice of 1 lemon
1 vanilla bean, halved lengthwise

Mix together all of the ingredients for the wafer cookies to form a smooth batter. Refrigerate for 30 minutes. Meanwhile, mix together the crushed strawberries, crème anglais and the gelatin. Heat the mixture in a saucepan to 105°F (40°C). Melt the chocolate and add it to the strawberry cream, stirring to incorporate completely. Beat the whipping cream to soft peaks and fold it into the strawberry cream little by little.

Refrigerate for 2 hours. Mix all the ingredients for the tartare together and set aside.

Preheat the oven to 350°F (180°C or Gas Mark 4). Spread the wafer batter into 1 by 5 inch (3 by 12 cm) rectangles on a baking sheet lined with parchment paper. Bake for a few minutes, until the wafers are golden-brown. Remove from the oven, and while still hot, roll the wafers around stainless-steel cannoli molds to form circles.

Spoon the strawberry tartare onto individual serving plates. Place a wafer cookie on top of the tartare and a spoonful of mousse inside the wafer. Serve immediately.

Preparation time **30 minutes**
Cooking time **15 minutes**
Level **difficult**

meringue, fig and white chocolate parfaits

Ingredients for 4 servings

Meringue:

2 oz (60 g) white chocolate

1/4 cup (60 ml) whipping cream

2 tbsps milk

1 egg white

4 meringues

6 ripe green figs

Melt the white chocolate over a double boiler with the cream and milk. Let cool slightly.
Beat the egg white and add it to the mixture.
Pour into a whipped cream canister (soda siphon), close, insert the gas cartridge and shake lightly.
Place the canister in a pan of hot water (175°F or 80°C) to keep warm.
Crumble the meringues into the bottom of 4 small glasses. Peel the figs and slice them into quarters using a paring knife. Place the fig quarters on top of the crushed meringues.
Top the parfaits with warm white chocolate foam and serve immediately.

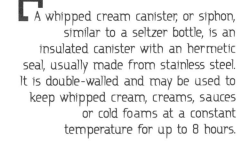

A whipped cream canister, or siphon, similar to a seltzer bottle, is an insulated canister with an hermetic seal, usually made from stainless steel. It is double-walled and may be used to keep whipped cream, creams, sauces or cold foams at a constant temperature for up to 8 hours.

Desserts

308

Preparation time **20 minutes**
Cooking time **10 minutes**
Level **medium**

white chocolate crème brûlée

Ingredients for 6 servings
Crème Brûlée:

1¾ cups (400 ml) whipping cream

1 vanilla bean, halved lengthwise

4½ oz (130 g) white chocolate

6 egg yolks

1/3 cup plus 1 tbsp (3 oz or 80 g) raw
cane sugar

Heat the cream and the vanilla bean in a small saucepan. Once the cream begins to simmer, remove from the heat, and using a small knife, scrape the seeds out of the vanilla bean and into the cream.
Melt the chocolate over a double boiler or in a microwave, stirring frequently. Remove from the heat and stir in the egg yolks one at a time.
Whisk in the hot cream, transfer the mixture to a saucepan and return to the stove. Cook the mixture until it begins to thicken and coats the back of a spoon.
Strain the mixture and pour it into 6 ramekins. Refrigerate overnight. Before serving, sprinkle the crème brûlées with raw cane sugar and caramelize the sugar using a kitchen torch or by placing the ramekins under a pre-heated broiler for a few minutes. Serve immediately.

A kitchen torch is a useful device
for caramelizing sugar or
flaming poultry.

Preparation time **25 minutes**
Cooking time **15 minutes**
Level **medium**

white chocolate and ginger sorbet

Ingredients for 4 servings

Sorbet:

3/4 cups plus 1 tbsp
(6 oz or 175 g) sugar

2 cups (500 ml) water

5½ oz (150 g) white
chocolate, chopped

1 tbsp freshly grated ginger

Decoration:

red currant sprigs

fresh ginger, julienned

Heat the sugar and water in a saucepan.
When the syrup begins to boil, remove from heat.
Add the chocolate and ginger, beating well with a whisk to obtain a smooth cream.
Return to the heat, stirring constantly, until the mixture comes to a simmer.
Place the saucepan in an ice water bath to cool quickly.
Pour into an ice cream machine and mix briefly.
Transfer the container to the freezer and leave overnight.
Serve the sorbet with redcurrants and strips of julienned ginger.

For a better sorbet consistency and texture, substitute 1/4 cup (2 oz or 50 g) of sugar with 3 tbsps glucose syrup.

Preparation time **20 minutes**
Cooking time **15 minutes**
Level **medium**

chocolate tiramisù

Ingredients for 4 servings

Tiramisù:

8 ladyfingers

7 tbsps egg liqueur (such as Vov)

3 oz (80 g) milk chocolate

4 tbsps whipping cream

4 egg yolks

2 tbsps sugar

1 tbsp sweet Marsala wine

2 oz (60 g) mascarpone

Garnish:

1 tbsp instant coffee

wafer cookies (optional)

Mascarpone pairs well with chocolate thanks to its thick consistency and high fat content.

Slice the ladyfingers in half and soak them in the egg liqueur. Line 4 glass bowls or cups with the ladyfingers. Meanwhile, melt the chocolate and cream over a double boiler or in the microwave. Let cool, and when tepid, pour the chocolate sauce over the ladyfingers.
Beat the egg yolks and the sugar in a round-bottomed bowl over a double boiler over medium heat.
When the mixture is thick and foamy, pour over the Marsala and continue beating until the mixture has tripled in volume. Remove from the heat and immerse the pan in a cold water bath to stop the cooking.
Fold in the mascarpone and spoon the sauce into the bowls or cups. Let sit for 5 minutes and then sprinkle with the instant coffee.
Decorate with wafer cookies if desired.

Preparation time **40 minutes**
Cooking time **20 minutes**
Level **easy**

double chocolate frappé

Ingredients for 4 servings

Frappé:

7 oz (200 g) white chocolate ice cream

20 ice cubes

3/4 cup (200 ml) milk

7 oz (200 g) milk chocolate ice cream

Decoration:

4 tbsps whipped cream

dark chocolate, shaved

Blend the white chocolate ice cream in a blender with half the ice cubes and half the milk.
Pour the mixture into 4 tall glasses.
Blend the milk chocolate ice cream with the remaining milk and ice cubes. Hold a spoon in the glass and pour the milk chocolate frappé over the spoon so it lands as gently as possible on top of the white chocolate frappé, creating two distinct layers.
Decorate with whipped cream and chocolate shavings.
Serve immediately

For a single color frappé, substitute the milk chocolate ice cream with 7 oz (200 g) of plain yogurt.

Preparation time **15 minutes**
Level **easy**

white chocolate sabayon
with mixed berries

Ingredients for 4 servings
Sabayon:
4 egg yolks
2 tbsps sugar
2½ oz (70 g) white chocolate
7 oz (200 g) mixed berries
(raspberries,strawberries,
blackberries, blueberries)

Beat the egg yolks and sugar over a double boiler.
Cook the mixture, stirring vigorously with a whisk.
Meanwhile melt the white chocolate.
Slowly pour the melted chocolate into the egg mixture
and continue beating until doubled in volume.
Place the berries in 4 martini glasses and top
with the white chocolate sabayon sauce.
Serve immediately.

For an elegant variation,
replace the white chocolate
with the same quantity
of dark chocolate.

Preparation time **20 minutes**
Cooking time **15 minutes**
Level **easy**

white chocolate pudding

Ingredients for 4 servings

Pudding:

1/3 cup plus 1 tbsp (2 oz or 55 g) all-purpose flour

6 cups (1½ l) whole milk

8 egg yolks

3 oz (80 g) white chocolate, chopped

1/2 cup plus 1 tbsp (4 oz or 115 g) vanilla sugar

Decoration:

mint leaves (optional)

Heat the flour and 1/2 cup (120 ml) milk in a saucepan over low heat. Whisk in the egg yolks one by one until fully incorporated.
Melt the chocolate over a double boiler.
Add the sugar and melted chocolate to the egg mixture and stir in the remaining milk.
Return to the heat and cook, stirring constantly, until the mixture just comes to a boil.
Pour into a pudding mold and let cool completely before serving. Decorate with mint leaves if desired.

320

This elegant pudding could be served on a plate decorated with chocolate sauce. For more color, garnish mixed berries or strawberries.

Preparation time **30 minutes**
Cooking time **30 minutes**
Level **easy**

mini milk chocolate charlottes

Ingredients for 4 servings

Charlottes:

4 tbsps orange-flower liqueur

20 ladyfingers

8 oz (230 g) milk chocolate

2/3 cup (150 ml) whipping cream

4 eggs, separated

salt

3/4 cup (5½ oz or 150 g) sugar

Line 4 mini spring-form pans with parchment paper.
Dilute the orange-flower liqueur with a few spoonfuls
of water and use the mixture to brush the ladyfingers.
Line the spring-form pans with the ladyfingers.
Melt the chocolate over a double boiler or in a microwave
and then stir in the whipping cream.
Beat the egg whites with a pinch of salt, slowly add
the sugar and continue beating to stiff peaks.
Whisk the egg yolks into the chocolate mixture one
at a time. Fold the egg whites into the chocolate mixture
and stir carefully to incorporate.
Pour the mixture into the spring-form pans and
refrigerate overnight.
Unmold before serving.

The ladyfingers may be
soaked in any liqueur,
or in coffee.

Preparation time **30 minutes**
Cooking time **5 minutes**
Level **easy**

chocolate roll

Ingredients for 6 servings

Cake:

3 eggs

3/4 cups plus 2 tbsps (5 oz or 135 g) sugar

4 tbsps all-purpose flour, sifted

1/4 cup (1 oz or 25 g) cocoa powder, sifted

Cream:

1¼ cups (300 ml) whipping cream

3½ oz (100 g) white chocolate

Preheat the oven to 400°F (200°C or Gas Mark 6). Using an electric beater with the whisk attachment, beat the eggs with 1/2 cup (3½ oz or 95 g) sugar. When the mixture lightens in color and begins to form ribbons, carefully fold in the sifted flour and cocoa powder. Pour the batter into a rectangular baking sheet lined with parchment paper. Spread the batter with a spatula to form a uniform layer. Bake for 15 minutes. Meanwhile, place a clean kitchen towel on a work surface and top with paper towels. Sprinkle the remaining sugar over the paper towels. Invert the hot sponge cake onto the paper towels androll up the sponge cake like a jelly roll. Meanwhile melt the white chocolate over a double boiler or in a microwave. Whip the whipping cream to stiff peaks and fold in the melted white chocolate. Unroll the sponge cake, spread the chocolate cream over the cake and re-roll the cake. Cover the cake and refrigerate until firm. Slice the chocolate roll and serve.

The white chocolate for the filling may be substituted with 2/3 cup (150 ml) of sweetened condensed milk.

Preparation time **20 minutes**
Cooking time **15 minutes**
Level **medium**

violet wafer cookies with milk chocolate ice cream and vanilla liqueur

Ingredients for 4 servings

Wafers:

1/4 cup (2 oz or 60 g) butter

2 egg whites

1/2 cup (2 oz or 60 g) confectioners' sugar

1/2 cup (2 oz or 60 g) all-purpose flour

1 tbsp dried violets

Decoration:

1/2 cup (120 ml) vanilla cream liqueur

10½ oz (300 g) milk chocolate ice cream

Preheat the oven to 400°F (200°C or Gas Mark 6).
Melt the butter and let it cool. Lightly beat the egg whites with the sugar. Add the butter and sift in the flour. Refrigerate for 20 minutes.
Line a baking sheet with parchment paper. Spread a small amount of batter on the sheet and smooth with the back of a spoon to form a circle.
Repeat to make a total of 4 wafers.
Sprinkle the dried violets over the wafers and bake for about 4 minutes, or until the edges begin to brown. Using a spatula, remove the hot wafers from the baking sheet and place them over inverted tea cups to form little cups. Freeze the vanilla liqueur for 30 minutes before serving. Pour the frozen liquor into shot glasses, place the wafer cup on top of the glass and top with a scoop of chocolate ice cream. Serve immediately.

If dried violets are unavailable, use candied violets to garnish the dessert.

Preparation time **30 minutes**
Cooking time **5 minutes**
Level **medium**

milk and white chocolate tiny treats

chocolate

eggplant and white chocolate mousse cups

Ingredients for 4 servings

Cups:

4 tbsps (2 oz or 50 g) butter

1 large eggplant, peeled and diced

1 tbsp confectioners' sugar

4 oz (120 g) white chocolate

2/3 cup (150 ml) whipping cream

1/3 cup (2 oz or 50 g) hazelnuts, toasted and chopped

10½ oz (300 g) shortcrust dough (see p. 386)

Eggplant is a versatile vegetable which can be used in both sweet and savory preparations. For a delicious eggplant jam, combine 1 lb (450 g) diced eggplant with 1 lb (450 g) sugar, 1 tbsp freshly grated ginger and the julienned zest of 2 lemons and 2 oranges. Cook over low heat for 2 hours, season with freshly chopped mint and cook for another 15 minutes.

Melt the butter in a heavy-bottomed saucepan.
Add the eggplant and sauté. Sprinkle with confectioners' sugar and cook over low heat for 15 minutes, until caramelized and soft. Puree the eggplant in a food processor and let cool.
Melt the chocolate in a microwave or over a double boiler. Beat the whipping cream to stiff peaks and fold it into the melted chocolate.
Fold in the eggplant puree and hazelnuts. Cover and refrigerate for 1 hour.
Meanwhile, preheat the oven to 375°F (190°C or Gas Mark 5). Butter and flour miniature muffin tins, quiche tins or boat-shaped molds and line with the shortcrust dough. Bake for 15 minutes, then let cool completely.
Fill the cups with the eggplant mousse and serve immediately.

Preparation time **30 minutes**
Cooking time **40 minutes**
Level **medium**

milk chocolate cupcakes

Ingredients for 6 servings

Cupcakes:

7 tbsps (3½ oz or 100 g) butter

3 eggs, separated, **1** tbsp honey

1/2 cup (3½ oz or 100 g) sugar

1 tsp vanilla extract

1/2 cup (1½ oz or 40 g) graham crackers, crushed

1/3 cup (1½ oz or 40 g) breadcrumbs

3 tbsp (45 ml) white rum

1/3 cup plus 1 tbsp (2 oz or 50 g) pistachios, finely chopped

Frosting:

9 oz (250 g) milk chocolate, chopped, salt

This recipe may be varied in many ways according to taste. The rum may be substituted with coffee or with coconut or orange liqueur.

Preheat the oven to 350°F (180°C or Gas Mark 4). Melt the butter and let cool. Beat the egg yolks and the sugar with the vanilla until thick and pale yellow. Whisk in the cooled butter. Add the graham crackers, breadcrumbs and rum and mix well.
Beat the egg whites and salt into stiff peaks and fold into the batter. Add the honey and chopped pistachios and stir to combine.
Butter and flour 6 aluminum ramequins or muffin tins and fill them two-thirds full with the batter.
Bake for 25 minutes, remove from the oven and let cool on a wire rack. Meanwhile, temper the chocolate with the salt (see p. 384). Spread the frosting on the cupcakes and let sit on a wire rack until hardened.

Preparation time **30 minutes**
Cooking time **40 minutes**
Level **medium**

soft hazelnut torrone

Ingredients for 4 servings

Torrone:

2 cups (14 oz or 400 g) sugar

7 oz (200 g) milk chocolate with hazelnuts, chopped

2½ oz (70 g) dark couverture chocolate, chopped

3/4 cup (10½ oz or 300 g) honey

3 egg whites

1¾ lb (800 g) hazelnuts

2 edible wafer paper sheets

Place 4 tablespoons sugar and 2½ tablespoons water in a small saucepan and heat until the sugar dissolves and forms a syrup. Transfer the syrup to a double boiler, add both types of chocolate and let melt. Meanwhile, place the honey in another small saucepan and heat until it forms a hard ball when dropped into a glass of water. Beat the egg whites to stiff peaks.
Caramelize the remaining sugar with 1/2 cup (120 ml) water and add it to the honey. Add the egg whites, chocolate mixture and the hazelnuts. Line a baking sheet with 1 sheet of edible wafer paper. Pour the torrone mixture onto the wafer paper and smooth with a spatula to form an even layer.
Cover with the second sheet of wafer paper and place another baking sheet on top, pressing down to form a layer 1/2 inch (1½ cm) thick.
Let the torrone harden and then cut into small rectangles. The torrone may then be wrapped in decorative paper and preserved in an air-tight container.

There are several types of honey available. The most widely used in baking is acacia honey, which has an amber color and delicate flavor. It is an excellent sweetener for drinks because it doesn't alter the original flavor.

Preparation time **20 minutes**
Cooking time **15 minutes**
Level **easy**

chocolate-hazelnut swirls

Ingredients for 20 cookies

Swirls:

5½ oz (150 g) milk chocolate

2/3 cup (150 ml) water

3 tsps chocolate-hazelnut cream
(such as Nutella)

3 tsps Cointreau

7 tbsps (3½ oz or 100 g) butter

confectioners' sugar

Melt the chocolate over a double boiler or in a microwave.
Heat the water, chocolate-hazelnut cream and Cointreau in a small saucepan.
When the mixture begins to simmer, pour it over the melted chocolate and whisk to combine.
Add the butter and mix to form a smooth cream.
Refrigerate the cream for 20 minutes.
Transfer the cream to a pastry bag fitted with a ridged tip.
Pipe out little puffs of the chocolate cream onto a baking sheet lined with parchment paper.
Refrigerate for 2 hours.
Sprinkle the chocolate-hazelnut swirls with confectioners' sugar. Refrigerate until serving.

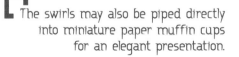
The swirls may also be piped directly into miniature paper muffin cups for an elegant presentation.

Preparation time **25 minutes**
Cooking time **10 minutes**
Level **easy**

mini walnut brownies

Ingredients for 22 brownies

Brownies:

4½ oz (125 g) milk chocolate

6 tbsps (3 oz or 90 g) butter

2½ cups (9 oz or 250 g) confectioners' sugar

1 tsp vanilla extract

2 eggs

2/3 cup (3 oz or 80 g) all-purpose flour

1/3 cup (1 oz or 30 g) cocoa powder

1/2 tsp baking powder

1 cup (4 oz or 120 g) walnuts, chopped

Preheat the oven to 350°F (180°C or Gas Mark 4).
Melt the chocolate over a double boiler or in a microwave.
Beat the butter, sugar and vanilla together using an electric mixer. Add the eggs and beat well
Stir in the melted chocolate. Sift in the flour, cocoa powder and baking powder. Mix gently with a spatula.
Add the nuts and stir to combine.
Pour the batter into a rectangular baking dish lined with parchment paper and smooth the top with a spatula.
Bake for 35 minutes.
Let cool and cut into small rectangles.
Serve the brownies in miniature paper baking cups.

Brownies are an American classic. Try serving them with hot with a scoop of vanilla ice cream for brownies à la mode.

Preparation time **30 minutes**
Cooking time **40 minutes**
Level **medium**

mini goat's milk cheesecakes

Ingredients for 4 servings

Cheesecakes:

2½ oz (70 g) white chocolate

8½ oz (240 g) fresh goat's cheese

6 tbsps whipping cream

1 cup plus 1 tbsp (4½ oz or 130 g) confectioners' sugar

1 egg, lightly beaten

4 chocolate wafer cookies

Decoration:

raspberries

mint leaves

Preheat the oven to 325°F (170°C or Gas Mark 3).

Melt the chocolate over a double boiler or in a microwave, stirring frequently.

Using an electric mixer, beat the cheese, whipping cream and confectioners' sugar until light and fluffy.

Add the egg and drizzle in the melted chocolate, stirring with a wooden spoon or spatula.

Line 4 ceramic ramequins with two overlapping strips of parchment paper. Place 1 wafer cookie in the bottom of each ramequin and fill two-thirds full with the cheese filling. Bake for 20 minutes.

Let cool completely and refrigerate for 1 hour.

Decorate the mini cheesecakes with raspberries and mint leaves.

If desired, the chocolate wafer cookies may be replaced with any other kind of cookie or 4 slices of any kind of chocolate cake.

Preparation time **20 minutes**
Cooking time **30 minutes**
Level **easy**

meringue and rum truffles

Ingredients for 4 servings

Truffles:

1/4 cup (60 ml) whipping cream

1 tsp white rum

7 oz (200 g) milk chocolate, finely chopped

2 oz (60 g) meringues

3 tbsps cocoa powder

Heat the cream and rum in a small saucepan.
Add the chocolate and whisk until the mixture is smooth.
Let cool in the refrigerator for 5 minutes, stirring at least 3 times, until the mixture begins to thicken.
Crush the meringues and add them to the chocolate mixture. Using the hands, form walnut-sized balls and place on a baking sheet.
Refrigerate for at least 15 minutes.
Once chilled, roll the truffles in the cocoa powder.
Keep the truffles in a cool place and serve at the end of a meal with dessert wines or liqueurs.

Meringues may be prepared at home using the following recipe: Beat 1 egg white and a pinch of salt until frothy. Slowly add 1/2 cup (3½ oz or 100 g) sugar and continue beating until the mixture forms stiff peaks and becomes glossy. Place the batter in a pastry bag and pipe out the meringues onto a baking sheet lined with parchment paper. Bake the meringues at 210°F (100°C or Gas Mark 1/4) for at least 1 hour 30 minutes.

Preparation time **25 minutes**
Cooking time **10 minutes**
Level **easy**

Tiny Treats

chocolate wafers with white chocolate cream

Ingredients for 4 servings

Wafers:

1 egg white, **2** tbsps cocoa powder

1/2 cup (2 oz or 60 g) confectioners' sugar

4 tbsps (2 oz or 60 g) melted butter

1/3 cup plus 1 tbsp (2 oz or 50 g) all-purpose flour

Cream:

2/3 cup (150 ml) milk

1½ oz (40 g) white chocolate

1 cup (250 ml) whipping cream

1 tbsp confectioners' sugar

Decoration:

1 oz (25 g) dark chocolate, shaved

This dessert can be made without a whipped cream canister. Whip the whipping cream to stiff peaks, then carefully fold in the melted chocolate and milk mixture. Transfer to a pastry bag and pipe the cream into the wafer cups.

Beat the egg white with the confectioners' sugar. Add the cooled melted butter and sift in the flour and cocoa powder.

Refrigerate the batter until cooled and thickened. Meanwhile, heat the milk in a saucepan and add the chocolate. Melt over medium heat, stirring frequently. Let cool slightly, add the confectioners' sugar and pour into a whipped cream canister (siphon).

Add the whipping cream to the canister, close and add the gas cartridge. Leave in a cool place.

Preheat the oven to 400°F (200°C or Gas Mark 6). Spread small spoonfuls of batter onto a baking sheet lined with parchment paper and spread the batter into thin rounds with the back of a spoon.

Bake for 4 minutes, then remove from the oven. Mold the hot wafers over the bottom of a demi-tasse cup or the neck of a bottle to form small cups.

When the wafer cups are cool, place them on individual serving plates and fill with the white chocolate cream. Garnish with dark chocolate shavings and serve immediately.

Preparation time **30 minutes**
Cooking time **8 minutes**
Level **easy**

mini chocolate cake squares
with strawberries

Ingredients for 4 servings
Chocolate cake:

3½ oz (100 g) milk chocolate

2 oz (50 g) dark chocolate

5 tbsps (2½ oz or 75 g) butter

2/3 cup (2½ oz or 75 g) sugar

1 tbsp brandy, **2** eggs, lightly beaten

3½ oz (100 g) mascarpone

1/3 cup (1½ oz or 40 g)
all-purpose flour

1 tbsp cornstarch

3/4 cup (2½ oz or 75 g) almonds,
toasted and ground

Decoration:

2 oz (50 g) white chocolate

1 basket of strawberries,
hulled and halved

This dessert may also be decorated
with seasonal berries such as
raspberries or blackberries.

Preheat the oven to 350°F (180°C or Gas Mark 4).
Melt the milk chocolate and dark chocolate over a double boiler or in a microwave.
Using an electric mixer, cream the butter and sugar
Add the chocolate, brandy, eggs and finally the mascarpone. Sift in the flour and cornstarch and add the ground almonds. Mix to combine and pour the batter into small rectangular tins or silicon molds.
Bake for 20 minutes and let cool completely.
Melt the white chocolate and let cool.
Unmold the chocolate cakes and place a dollop of melted white chocolate on top of each cake.
Top with a strawberry half. Let cool completely and serve.

Preparation time **30 minutes**
Cooking time **25 minutes**
Level **easy**

white chocolate log

Ingredients for 8 servings

Log:

9 oz (250 g) white chocolate

7 tbsps (3½ oz or 100 g) butter, softened

1/2 cup (3½ oz or 100 g) sugar

2 egg yolks

1/4 cup (60 ml) espresso coffee

10½ oz (300 g) graham crackers, crushed

1 handful of mixed nuts (almonds, walnuts, hazelnuts), chopped

Decoration:

raspberries

mint leaves

Melt the chocolate over a double boiler and let cool slightly. Cream the butter and sugar and add the egg yolks one at a time. Drizzle in the chocolate and mix well.
Add the coffee and crushed graham crackers and stir well. Finally, add the nuts, stirring with a wooden spoon. Place the mixture in the center of a large sheet of aluminum foil.
Form a log and roll up the aluminum foil, twisting the ends like a candy wrapper to seal. Refrigerate for 2 hours.
Slice the log thickly and garnish with raspberries and mint leaves.

This dessert pairs well with sweet Asti Spumante Moscato wine.

Preparation time **15 minutes**
Cooking time **5 minutes**
Level **easy**

chocolate beignets with white chocolate mousse

Ingredients for 4 servings

Beignets:

3/4 cup (175 ml) water

5 tbsps (2½ oz or 75 g) butter, salt

3/4 cups plus 1 tbsp (3½ oz or 100 g)
all-purpose flour

1/2 cup plus 1 tbsp (2 oz or 50 g)
cocoa powder

1/4 cup (2 oz or 50 g) sugar, **2** eggs

Mousse:

7 oz (200 g) white chocolate

2 gelatin sheets, **1** egg plus 1 egg yolk

2/3 cup (4 oz or 120 g) sugar

2/3 cup (150 ml) whipping cream

Preheat the oven to 400°F (200°C or Gas Mark 6).
Bring the water and butter to a boil with a pinch of salt.
Sift together the flour, cocoa powder and sugar.
When the water boils, add the flour mixture and stir
vigorously with a wooden spoon until the mixture begins
to pull away from the sides of the pan. Remove from the
heat and add the eggs one at a time, stirring constantly.
Return to heat and cook for 1 minute.
Transfer the dough to a pastry bag and make small puffs
on a baking sheet lined with parchment paper.
Bake for 20 minutes, remove from the oven and cool
on a wire rack. Melt the white chocolate for the mousse
over a double boiler.
Soak the gelatin sheets in cold water for a few minutes.
Drain and squeeze out the excess water. Beat the egg
and egg yolk with the sugar and add the gelatin.
Beat the whipping cream to stiff peaks and fold it
into the egg mixture. Refrigerate until firm.
Slice the beignets in half and fill them with the white
chocolate mousse.

These beignets may also be filled with
the following cream: Puree 1 basket of
raspberries with 2 tablespoons sugar. Whip
3/4 cup (200 ml) whipping cream until
quite stiff, then fold in the raspberry puree.

Preparation time **30 minutes**
Cooking time **20 minutes**
Level **medium**

black and white cookies

Ingredients for 4 servings

Cookies:

3 cups (13 oz or 370 g) all-purpose flour

1¼ cups (9 oz or 250 g) sugar

3/4 cup (7 oz or 200 g) butter, softened

3 eggs

salt

1 tsp vanilla extract

1 oz (30 g) milk chocolate

Sift the flour into a bowl. Add the sugar, softened butter, 2 eggs, a pinch of salt and the vanilla. Mix well to obtain a smooth dough.

Melt the chocolate over a double boiler or in a microwave. Add the chocolate to half of the dough, kneading until the chocolate is incorporated. Wrap the two doughs in plastic wrap and refrigerate for 30 minutes.

Preheat the oven to 350°F (180°C or Gas Mark 4).

Roll out each piece of dough with a rolling pin to a 1/4-inch (1 cm) thickness. Cut the dough into several strips.

Line a baking tray with parchment paper and place 1 strip of chocolate dough next to 1 strip of plain dough, slightly overlapping the edge. Make a second layer on top of the first, taking care to alternate the types of dough.

Brush with the remaining egg and slice the double layer strips into square cookies. They should look like miniature chess boards. Place the cookies on a baking sheet and bake for 10 minutes. Let cool completely on a wire rack and serve with a light pastry cream and tea.

These cookies, accompanied by light hot chocolate, make a perfect snack for young children

Preparation time **20 minutes**
Cooking time **10 minutes**
Level **easy**

hazelnut chocolates

Ingredients for 6 servings

Chocolates:

1/3 cup (50 g) blanched hazelnuts

5½ oz (150 g) white chocolate

5½ oz (150 g) milk chocolate

Toast the hazelnuts in the oven or in a pan on the stove over high heat for 5 minutes.
Meanwhile, melt the 2 types of chocolate separately.
Fold a rectangular piece of parchment paper into a cone and fill the cone with the melted white chocolate.
Cut the tip of the cone to make a small hole.
Pipe a little white chocolate into the bottom of a silicon mold for chocolates. Chill for 10 minutes.
Pour the milk chocolate over the chilled white chocolate and place one hazelnut in each chocolate.
Level off the mold with a spatula and let harden in the refrigerator for another 10 minutes.
Unmold the chocolates and serve in mini paper baking cups.

Similar chocolates may be made using dark chocolate in the place of the milk chocolate and toasted almonds in the place of hazelnuts.

Preparation time **20 minutes**
Cooking time **20 minutes**
Level **easy**

miniature chocolate diplomat cakes

Ingredients for 6 servings

Cake:

8 oz (220 g) milk chocolate

6½ oz (180 g) dark chocolate

2 eggs plus 2 egg yolks

1¼ cups (8½ oz or 240 g) sugar

4 gelatin sheets

1¼ cups (300 ml) whipping cream

1 lb (500 g) sponge cake (see p. 386)

1/2 cup (120 ml) rum

Decoration:

confectioners' sugar

milk chocolate

Melt the 2 types of chocolate over separate double boilers.
Beat the eggs and egg yolks with the sugar until thick and pale yellow.
Soak the gelatin in cold water, drain and squeeze out the excess water. Place 2 sheets in each type of melted chocolate and stir to combine. Divide the egg yolk mixture between the chocolate mixtures.
Beat the whipping cream to stiff peaks and divide it between the chocolate mixtures, folding it in gently.
Slice the sponge cake into long rectangular strips and brush them with the rum diluted with a little water.
Spread the milk chocolate cream over one strip of sponge cake and top it with another strip of cake.
Repeat using the dark chocolate cream.
Refrigerate for 2 hours.
Cut the cake into small rectangles, sprinkle with confectioners' sugar and top with chocolate shavings.

The sponge cake may be softened with milk instead of rum if desired.

Preparation time **20 minutes**
Cooking time **5 minutes**
Level **medium**

white chocolate cupcakes

Ingredients for 4 servings

Cupcakes:

9 tbsps (4½ oz or 125 g) butter

3/4 cup plus 1 tbsp (6½ oz or 180 g) sugar

2 eggs, **1** tsp vanilla extract

2 cups (9 oz or 250 g) self-rising flour

1/2 cup (110 ml) whipping cream

9 oz (250 g) white chocolate, shaved

Frosting:

3½ oz (100 g) cream cheese

2½ tbsps confectioners' sugar

2 oz (50 g) white chocolate

2 tbsps whipping cream

Preheat the oven to 325°F (170°C or Gas Mark 3).
Cream the butter and sugar together in a mixer.
Add the eggs one at a time and then the vanilla.
Sift in the flour, stirring with a spatula, and then add the whipping cream. Mix in the chocolate shavings.
Fill miniature muffin tins or babà molds with the batter until half full. Bake for 20 minutes. Let cool, then unmold.
Whip the cream cheese with the confectioners' sugar.
Melt the chocolate with the whipping cream and add to the cream cheese mixture.
Frost the cupcakes with the white chocolate frosting and let sit for 10 minutes before serving.

For a darker variation, substitute the white chocolate in the frosting with the same quantity of milk or dark chocolate.

Preparation time **30 minutes**
Cooking time **20 minutes**
Level **easy**

Tangy Treats

chocolate cupcakes
with white chocolate glaze

Ingredients for 12 cupcakes

Cupcakes:

1½ cups (7 oz or 200 g) blanched hazelnuts

13 tbsps (6½ oz or 180 g) butter

6 egg whites

1¼ cups (5½ oz or 155 g) all-purpose flour

1/3 cup (1 oz or 30 g) cocoa powder

2½ cups (9 oz or 250 g) confectioners' sugar

Glaze:

3 oz (80 g) white chocolate

Preheat the oven to 400°F (200°C or Gas Mark 6).
Finely chop the hazelnuts in a food processor.
Melt the butter in a small saucepan, letting it brown slightly, for about 4 minutes. Let cool. Beat the egg whites to stiff peaks.
Sift together the flour, cocoa powder and confectioners' sugar. Add the hazelnuts and stir to combine.
Fold in the egg whites and then the melted butter.
Mix well and transfer to 12 miniature muffin tins, filling each tin half full. Bake for 20-25 minutes, using a toothpick make sure the cake is cooked through.
Remove from the oven and let cool completely.
Melt the white chocolate over a double boiler over low heat. When the first pieces begin to melt, remove from heat and stir until liquid.
Transfer the white chocolate to a pastry bag fitted with a small tip and decorate the cupcakes.
Let the glaze set before serving.

In alternative to a pastry bag, make a cone out of parchment paper, fill it with the glaze and cut a small hole in the tip.

Preparation time **20 minutes**
Cooking time **30 minutes**
Level **easy**

chocolate ice cream truffles

Ingredients for 4 servings

Truffles:

14 oz (400 g) milk chocolate ice cream

5½ oz (150 g) dark chocolate,
finely chopped

1 cup (3 oz or 80 g) cocoa powder

Place a baking sheet or tray in the freezer for at least
30 minutes.
Using an ice cream scoop make small balls of ice cream
and place them on the cold baking sheet.
Return to the freezer
Meanwhile, melt two-thirds of the chocolate over a double
boiler, stirring constantly. When the chocolate becomes
liquid, add the remaining chocolate.
Remove from heat and cool until tepid but still liquid.
Sift the cocoa powder into a bowl. Using a toothpick, pick
up the ice cream balls one at a time and quickly immerse
them in the melted chocolate.
Remove from the chocolate, let some of the chocolate
drip off, and then roll in the cocoa powder.
Place on the baking sheet and return to the freezer
until serving.

Tiny Treats

⌐ This recipe is a perfect base
for experimentation. Use the ice
cream flavor of choice and
proceed with the recipe.

Preparation time **15 minutes**
Cooking time **5 minutes**
Level **easy**

mini chocolate cakes with white chocolate frosting and currants

Ingredients for 4 servings

Cakes:

1/2 cup (75 g) almonds

3½ oz (100 g) milk chocolate

2 oz (50 g) dark chocolate

5 tbsps (2½ oz or 75 g) butter

1/3 cup (2½ oz or 75 g) sugar

1 tbsp brandy, 2 eggs, 1 tbsp cornstarch

3½ oz (100 g) mascarpone

1/3 cup (1½ oz or 40 g) all-purpose flour

Decoration:

white chocolate mousse (see p. 350)

red and white currants

Preheat the oven to 325°F (170°C or Gas Mark 3). Toast the almonds in the oven until they begin to color and smell nutty. Let cool and then grind in a food processor.

Raise the oven temperature to 350°F (180°C or Gas Mark 4). Melt the milk and dark chocolate together over a double boiler.

Cream the butter and sugar in a mixer and add the chocolate, brandy, eggs and finally the mascarpone. Stir in the almonds and sift in the flour and cornstarch. Pour the batter into small rectangular molds.

Bake for about 20 minutes and let cool completely. Decorate the cakes with white chocolate mousse and fresh currants.

364

Toasting is a cooking technique that heats an ingredient without using any type of condiment (oil, butter etc.). It may be done in the oven, broiler or on the stove using a non-stick pan.

Preparation time **30 minutes**
Cooking time **20 minutes**
Level **easy**

white chocolate cookies

Ingredients for 4 servings

Cookies:

9 tbsps (4½ oz or 125 g) butter

2/3 cups (4½ oz or 125 g) sugar

2 egg yolks, **1** tsp baking soda

1 vanilla bean, halved lengthwise

1¼ cups (5½ oz or 155 g) all-purpose flour

3/4 cups (4 oz or 110 g) finely ground cornmeal

1/3 cup (2 oz or 60 g) chocolate chips

Decoration:

confectioners' sugar (optional)

Cream the butter and sugar, then add the egg yolks and the seeds from the vanilla bean. Sift in the flour, cornmeal and baking soda.
Mix to combine, taking care not to overwork the dough.
Flatten the dough into a disk and wrap in plastic wrap. Refrigerate for at least 1 hour.
Preheat the oven to 320°F (160°C or Gas Mark 3).
Divide the dough into 4 portions and mix the chocolate chips into each portion.
Roll out the dough on a lightly floured surface and cut out cookies using the cutters of choice.
Place the cookies on a baking sheet lined with parchment paper and bake for about 15 minutes. Cool on wire racks and sprinkle, if desired, with confectioners' sugar.

This is a good basic recipe that may be varied according to taste and desire. Try adding 5 tablespoons raisins or 4 tablespoons shredded coconut.

Preparation time **30 minutes**
Cooking time **15 minutes**
Level **easy**

armagnac chocolates

Ingredients for 8 servings
Filling:

1 cup (250 ml) whipping cream

4 tbsps (2 oz or 60 g) butter

9 oz (250 g) milk chocolate, chopped

1/2 cup (100 ml) Armagnac
or coffee liqueur

Coating:

7 oz (200 g) dark chocolate

2 oz (60 g) milk chocolate

Bring the cream and butter to a boil, remove from heat and transfer to a stainless-steel bowl.
Add the chocolate and the Armagnac and beat with a whisk to obtain a smooth cream. Pour the mixture into a silicon chocolate mold and refrigerate for at least 2 hours.
Meanwhile, melt the dark chocolate over a double boiler. Remove the chocolates from the refrigerator and unmold them. Place on a wire rack and pour the cooled dark chocolate over them. Return the chocolate pralines to the refrigerator to harden.
Melt the milk chocolate over a double boiler or in a microwave and transfer to a pastry bag fitted with a thin tip. Decorate the chocolates with the milk chocolate. Let sit briefly before serving.

Tiny Treats

A double boiler, or bain-marie, is a bowl or pan sitting on top of another pan of boiling water. This method is used for melting or gently cooking.

Preparation time **40 minutes**
Cooking time **10 minutes**
Level **difficult**

white chocolate-hazelnut cookies

Ingredients for 20 cookies

Cookies:

9 tbsps (4½ oz or 125 g) butter

2/3 cup (4½ oz or 125 g) sugar

2 egg yolks

1¼ cups (5½ oz or 155 g) all-purpose flour

3/4 cups (4 oz or 110 g) finely ground cornmeal

1½ oz (40 g) white chocolate, finely chopped

1 tsp baking soda

Decoration:

20 hazelnuts

Cream the butter and sugar together and add the egg yolks. Sift in the flour and cornmeal.
Add the baking soda and stir to combine, without over mixing. Flatten the dough into a disk and cover with plastic wrap. Refrigerate for at least 1 hour.
Preheat the oven to 325°F (170°C or Gas Mark 3).
Add the white chocolate to the dough and return to the refrigerator for a few minutes.
Roll out the dough on a lightly floured surface. Cut out the cookies using any kind of cutter and place a hazelnut in the center of each cookie.
Bake for 20 minutes on a baking sheet lined with parchment paper. Let cool completely before serving.

370

Piedmontese hazelnuts are considered to be some of the best in the world and are known for their aromatic qualities. The highest quality variety is called the "tonda gentile" and comes from the Langhe region.

Preparation time **30 minutes**
Cooking time **20 minutes**
Level **easy**

mixed berry tarts
with white chocolate cream

Ingredients for 4 servings

Tarts:

10½ oz (300 g) shortcrust dough (see p. 386)

7 oz (200 g) white chocolate mousse (see p. 350), chilled

5½ oz (150 g) mixed berries

Decoration:

1 tbsp simple sugar syrup

1 tbsp confectioners' sugar

mint leaves

Preheat the oven to 350°F (180°C or Gas Mark 4). Roll out the dough and use it to line 4 buttered and floured miniature tart tins.
Cover the tarts with aluminum foil and place a few dried beans or pie weights in the bottom of each one.
Bake for 15 minutes. Remove the foil and beans and let cool. Unmold the tarts and fill with the chilled white chocolate cream. Top with the berries and sprinkle with the simple sugar syrup.
Just before serving, sift a little confectioners' sugar over each tart and decorate with mint leaves.

To save time, both the shortcrust dough and white chocolate cream may be prepared in advance.

Preparation time **20 minutes**
Cooking time **15 minutes**
Level **easy**

chocolate-hazelnut cups with raisins

Ingredients for 4 servings

Hazelnut Cups:

1/2 cup (3 oz or 80 g) raisins

1/4 cup (60 ml) sweet Marsala wine

7 oz (200 g) milk chocolate, chopped

1 tbsp sesame oil

1/2 cup (2 oz or 60 g) blanched hazelnuts

cocoa powder

Soak the raisins in the Marsala. Place two-thirds of the chocolate over a double boiler. When the chocolate begins to melt, remove from heat and stir in the remaining chocolate and the sesame oil.

Toast the hazelnuts in the oven or in a non-stick frying pan. Let cool and finely chop with a sharp knife.

Drain the raisins and roll them in the cocoa powder.

Fill paper baking cups half full with the chocolate mixture. Drop one cocoa-covered raisin into each cup and cover with chocolate.

Top with the hazelnuts and refrigerate until serving.

The sesame oil may be substituted with sunflower oil and the raisins with small seedless grapes.

Preparation time **30 minutes**
Cooking time **10 minutes**
Level **easy**

hazelnut pralines

Ingredients for 4 servings

Pralines:

3/4 cup (3½ oz or 100 g) blanched hazelnuts

5½ oz (150 g) milk chocolate, chopped

2 tbsps whipping cream, at room temperature

Toast the hazelnuts in the oven or in a non-stick frying pan. Let cool and coarsely chop.
Heat two-thirds of the chocolate over a double boiler. When it begins to melt, add the remaining chocolate. Stir until smooth. Add the hazelnuts and the whipping cream. Stir to combine and pour the mixture into rectangular silicon chocolate molds or into a baking dish. Cover with plastic wrap and refrigerate until firm.
Unmold the pralines, or if using a baking dish cut into small squares.

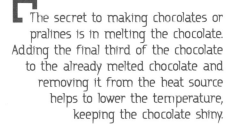
The secret to making chocolates or pralines is in melting the chocolate. Adding the final third of the chocolate to the already melted chocolate and removing it from the heat source helps to lower the temperature, keeping the chocolate shiny.

Preparation time **30 minutes**
Cooking time **15 minutes**
Level **easy**

baked hazelnut truffles

Ingredients for 20 truffles

Truffles:

1 oz (30 g) milk chocolate

4 tbsps (2 oz or 60 g) butter, softened

1 cup (6½ oz or 185 g) sugar

1/2 tsp vanilla extract

1 egg, lightly beaten

1⅔ cups (7 oz or 200 g)
all-purpose flour

1/2 tsp baking powder

1/3 cup (1½ oz or 40 g)
ground hazelnuts

confectioners' sugar

Melt the chocolate over a double boiler. Cream
the softened butter, sugar and vanilla in a mixer
or with an electric beater. Add the egg yolk and melted
chocolate. Sift in the flour and baking powder
and continue mixing. Finally add the hazelnuts.
Refrigerate the dough for 3 hours.
Preheat the oven to 350°F (180°C or Gas Mark 4).
Break off small pieces of the truffle dough and, using
the hands, roll it into balls.
Roll the truffles in the confectioners' sugar and place
them on a buttered baking sheet. Bake for 25 minutes.
Remove from the oven and cool completely.
Sprinkle with more confectioners' sugar, if desired.

These truffles may be made using
other types of nuts in place of the
hazelnuts. If desired, omit the nuts
completely and add 1 tablespoon of
rum to give greater flavor.

Preparation time **30 minutes**
Cooking time **30 minutes**
Level **easy**

basic techniques

chocolate

COOKING WITH CHOCOLATE

This section offers the home cook tips and suggestions for working with chocolate from some of the world's best pastry chefs and chocolatiers.

This advice will help ensure success when cooking with chocolate, as will using the highest quality ingredients, and using a candy thermometer in order to precisely control temperatures.

Preparing the Chocolate

When making chocolate candies, glazes, or other decorations, the first step is to prepare the chocolate. This preparation can require an infinite number of utensils, appliances and tools, given that the varied uses for chocolate are nearly infinite.

The following tools are fundamental for the most basic chocolate preparation: a small plastic chopping board, very sharp chef's knife, heat-resistant (Pyrex) storage containers, spatulas, graters, candy thermometer and spoons in metal and wood. These tools are helpful for preparing both complex and simple chocolate desserts.

Silicon molds are useful when working with chocolate. Many sizes and shapes are available and can be used in a variety of ways, both for baking and decorative purposes.

All of these tools can be used for preparations involving dark or milk chocolate. Once it has been melted over a double boiler, poured onto an plastic cutting board, uniformly spread using a spatula to a $1/2$ -inch (1 cm) thick layer, it is ready to be used in any way desired, with the only limit being your imagination.

an idea
Try a tasting of spirits (cognac, Armagnac, grappa, brandy, calvados, whisky, absinthe, etc.) paired with chocolate for an intense sensory experience.

Melting Chocolate...

The best way to melt chocolate is by using the water-bath method, also known as a double boiler or bain-marie.

Chop the chocolate and place it in a heat-resistant bowl or the top part of a double boiler pan. Place the bowl or pan over the base pan of the double boiler or another pot half-filled with water, making sure that the top bowl or pan is not touching the water. Bring the water to a simmer, without it reaching a full boil, and keep the temperature constant.

When the chocolate begins to melt, stir it with a wooden spoon until completely melted and smooth. In order to prevent lumps from forming, make sure that the chocolate is chopped or broken into evenly sized pieces before melting it. This will ensure that the chocolate pieces all melt at the same rate. It is important to remember that the melting point for chocolate depends on the size of the pieces of chocolate to be melted, the heat (high heat is not recommended) and the type of chocolate.

A microwave may also be used for melting chocolate. Remember to chop the chocolate into very small pieces and use a medium power setting.

...and Hardening Chocolate

Sometimes when preparing a ganache or chocolate decoration, the chocolate must be solidified, or hardened, and returned to a solid state. This will happen when the chocolate is cooled to around 64°F (18°C).

When hardening chocolate make sure to let the chocolate cool at room temperature. Never put it in the freezer as this can cause a white film to form on the surface.

tip
When melting chocolate in the microwave, lightly butter the bowl before placing the chopped chocolate in it.
We suggest about 2 minutes on high heat to melt a 3½ oz (100 g) bar of dark chocolate. It is advisable to lower the heat to medium when melting white or milk chocolate.

Grating and Chopping Chocolate

These are simple operations but require a little thought and preparation. Because chocolate melts easily it helps to refrigerate it for a few minutes before use. When grating chocolate, use a grater with larger holes. Remember to handle the chocolate as little as possible to avoid heating or melting. Grate the chocolate over a piece of parchment paper so it may be easily transferred to a cool place.

Tempering Chocolate

This procedure is particularly suitable for couverture chocolate, which is a kind of chocolate used to decorate cakes and other confectionery.

Couverture must be tempered so that when it dries and hardens, it is shiny and evenly colored, with no white bloom.

Cocoa butter tends to crystallize in an irregular way and so it is important to let melted chocolate cool slowly, to avoid it becoming cloudy or lumpy.

In scientific terms chocolate is a dispersion of crystalline sugar and cocoa powder in cocoa butter.

Tempering helps obtain a fine, regular crystallization of the cocoa butter. The difficulty of the process lies in the fact that sugar is water soluble while cocoa butter is hydrophobic or non-water soluble. Only the correct series of heating and cooling steps will result in shiny and malleable chocolate.

To temper chocolate, first melt the chocolate, stirring until the mixture is smooth and liquid, and has a temperature of 110°F (45°C). A candy thermometer is essential here.

Pour three-quarters of the chocolate onto a marble work surface or plastic cutting board and spread the liquid out with a stainless steel or plastic

an idea
For exquisite chocolate-covered candied orange rind, make sure that the white orange pith is removed before treating the rind. After glazing the strips of orange rind, they should be left to dry for a few days before coating with chocolate.

spatula. Continue to work the chocolate for a few minutes, making sure to fold it over itself, until the chocolate reaches 80°F (27°C).

At this point the chocolate with be partially solidified. Return the chocolate to the double boiler, stirring with a spatula to combine.

Heat to 91°F (32°C), making sure that the chocolate is bright and shiny. Leave the tempered chocolate in the double boiler and use immediately.

Tip: In order to perfectly temper the chocolate, it is important that the room temperature be between 68° and 70°F (20°-22°C), with humidity below 50%.

If you are planning to do a lot of work with chocolate, it may be worth investing in a professional tempering machine, available in specialty stores. In this case, place the chocolate in the container, turn on the machine and wait for the process to finish. The only disadvantage to this machine is its high cost.

Storing Chocolate

Finally, a word of advice on storing chocolate. Most commercially sold chocolate should keep for up to 1 year. Store it in a cool dry place in a plastic bag. Freezing chocolate is not recommended; not only does it alter the color of the chocolate, the flavor can also change.

Basic Pastry Recipes

Here are a few of the more basic pastry recipes used for preparing cakes, tarts and puddings in this book. While homemade pastry is delicious, when short on time, many high quality pastry crusts and cakes are available at supermarkets and specialty stores.

did you know....
Experts believe that hazelnut chocolate (about 543 calories per 3½ oz or 100 g) is not only crunchy and delicious but a healthy treat. It is rich in polyunsaturated fats that protect the heart. This type of chocolate may be prepared at home. Melt and solidify dark chocolate. Re-melt the chocolate in a double boiler and stir in blanched hazelnuts. Shape as desired.

Shortcrust Pastry

Ingredients for 14 oz (400 g) dough

1²⁄₃ cups (7 oz or 200 g) all-purpose flour; **7** tbsps (3½ oz or 100 g) butter, softened; **1/2** cup (3½ oz or 100 g) sugar; **2** egg yolks; grated zest of **1/2** organic lemon; salt

Method

Mound the flour on a work surface and make a well in the center. Add the butter, sugar, egg yolks, lemon zest and a pinch of salt to the well. Quickly mix the ingredients together.

When the dough is smooth and elastic, form a ball and cover with plastic wrap. Refrigerate for 1 hour. Remember to work quickly with the shortcrust pastry, touching it as little as possible.

Sponge Cake

Ingredients for 14 oz (400 g) cake

3/4 cup plus 1 tbsp (3½ oz or 100 g) all-purpose flour; **2/3** cup (3 oz or 80 g) cornstarch; **6** eggs, separated; 1²⁄₃ cups (7 oz or 200 g) confectioners' sugar; **1/2** tsp vanilla extract; butter

Method

Preheat the oven to 375°F (190°C or Gas Mark 5). Sift the flour and cornstarch into a mixing bowl. Beat the egg yolks with the sugar and vanilla until thick and foamy. Beat the egg whites to stiff peaks and carefully fold them into the egg yolk mixture.

a suggestion

Chefs advise using confectioners' sugar in place of granulated sugar when making chocolate creams or mousses, as the finely ground sugar dissolves easily. Adding cornstarch helps to bind all of the ingredients together.

Slowly add the flour mixture to the egg mixture, stirring with a wooden spoon until all of the flour has been incorporated.

Butter and flour an 8-inch (20 cm) cake pan. Pour in the batter and bake for 40 minutes. Remove from the oven and let cool completely. When cool, the sponge cake is ready for further use.

European Sponge Cake or Biscuit

Ingredients for 14 oz (400 g) cake

5 eggs, separated; **3/4** cup (5 oz or 150 g) sugar; **1** cup (4½ oz or 125 g) all-purpose flour; **1/4** cup (1 oz or 30 g) cornstarch; grated zest of **1** organic lemon; salt; butter

Method

Preheat the oven to 400°F (200°C or Gas Mark 6). Beat the egg yolks with the sugar until thick and foamy. Sift in the flour and cornstarch and add the lemon zest. Beat the egg whites and a pinch of salt to stiff peaks and fold them into the egg yolk mixture.

Line a rimmed baking sheet with greaseproof paper and pour in the batter. Using a spatula, spread the batter into a layer 1/2 inch (1 cm) thick.

Bake for 15 minutes and let cool completely before using.

For filled, rolled cakes: Invert the hot cake onto a damp kitchen towel and roll the cake up tightly. When cool, unroll the cake, fill it and re-roll.

advice

It is no secret that the flavor of chocolate is enhanced when infused with certain essences and spices like vanilla, the seed pod of a tropical flower belonging to the orchid family.

Many types and qualities of processed vanilla extracts and powders are readily available in supermarkets and specialty stores, but whole dried vanilla beans will give the richest and most authentic flavor.

basic tools

Chocolate

1 **Silicon Spatula** Indispensable for scraping batter out of pans and bowls. A silicon spatula is malleable and will mold to the form of the container.

2 **Mug** A ceramic cup, larger and thicker than a tea cup, ideal for sipping hot chocolate as well as coffee, tea or cappuccino. The thick walls of the cup keep liquids hot for longer periods and maintain the beverage's aromas.

3 **Cocoa Sifter** A small sifter used for uniformly dusting cocoa powder or confectioners' sugar over the top of a dessert.

4 **Ceramic Double Boiler** Useful for melting chocolate. The ceramic top pot helps to maintain a constant temperature and to keep the melted chocolate warm for longer periods of time.

5 **Electric Double Boiler** Melts and keeps chocolate warm, useful for making delicious chocolate fondue, in which can be dipped cookies or fresh fruit.

6 **Pastry Brushes** Evenly distribute liquids over a surface. When making chocolates brushes can be used to create a marbled effect.

7 **Whisks** Used for beating, whipping or emulsifying preparations. Whisks come in many sizes and shapes designed for specific uses.

Basic Tools

6

7

8

9

10

8 **Pastry Bag** Used to pipe semi-liquid foods by pressing them through a small opening fitted with a tip. Pastry bags are used for decorating any number of desserts.

9 **Serving Spatula** Indispensable for flipping, serving or spreading, these spatulas are made in many shapes and sizes and from a variety of materials, most commonly metal and plastic.

10 **Molds** Individual molds can come in many different shapes, sizes and materials and are used for sweet and savory tarts, flans and cakes.

11 **Chinois Sieve** A fine, conical sieve for straining creams or other thin liquids. The shape allows the liquid to be sieved directly into a small bowl or pan.

12 **Strainer** Kitchen tool made of a wire or nylon mesh of varying thickness, used to filter liquids, or to separate solids from liquids.

13 **Stainless Steel Mixing Bowls** Perfect for mixing any type of batter or dough, even with electric beaters. Stainless steel doesn't absorb or give off odors.

14 **Silicon Molds** Useful for shaping creams, mousses or chocolates. Frozen preparations are easily unmolded due to the flexibility of the silicon.

15 **Raised Serving Bowl** The perfect container for elegantly presenting puddings or mousses.

index

chocolate

Chocolate

Index

397

Index

Index

FIRESIDE

Fireside
A Division of Simon & Schuster, Inc.
1230 Avenue of the Americas
New York, NY 10020

Published originally under the title *Cioccolato & Co.*
Copyright © 2005 Food Editore srl
Via Bordoni, 8 - 20124 MILAN
Via Mazzini, 6 - 43100 PARMA
www.foodeditore.it

English Translation by
Traduzioni Culinarie

Photographs by
Alberto Rossi and Davide Di Prato

Recipes by
Simone Rugiati and Licia Cagnoni

First Fireside hardcover edition September 2008

FIRESIDE and colophon are registered trademarks of Simon & Schuster, Inc.

For information about special discounts for bulk purchases, please contact Simon & Schuster Special Sales
at 1-800-456-6798 or business@simonandschuster.com.

Printed in China

10 9 8 7 6 5 4 3 2 1

ISBN-13: 978-1-4165-9342-3
ISBN-10:   1-4165-9342-X